The Road Chose Me Volume 1

Two years and 40,000 miles from Alaska to Argentina

Dan Grec

THE ROAD CHOSE ME

For Mum and Dad.

When I was young, you said I could do anything.
And I believed you.

You were right.

Route through the Americas

Contents

Introduction

Bamako, West Africa, Mali
September 2016

W HEN I set out to drive my little Jeep Wrangler from Alaska to Argentina, I had no idea how much the journey would change my life. I had no idea the people I would meet, the experiences I would have and the lessons I would learn could have such a deep and lasting impact.

I thought I was just going for a drive, but it turned into so much more. I will never be the same person, and the course of my life has been altered permanently. I can never go back to who I was or what I was doing before, so strong was the impact of the experiences that came my way.

During the journey I posted stories and photos of my adventures on my website. Through the site, I was able to show friends and family what I was doing. To my surprise, many people I had never met also joined the adventure and followed along. I was shocked when complete strangers reached out to say how my adventures were inspiring them to get out and live their own dreams.

It has taken many years to write this book. That's because it has taken many years to fully understand the lessons I learned during the journey. This book contains my stories of adventures, experiences and the fascinating people I met. More importantly, it contains the major lessons I learned on the road. Life in Latin America is unlike the one I knew, and I was able to learn from many people who see things in a completely different way than I had ever known.

I hope this book inspires you to go out and have adventures of your own. I also hope you can take in the lessons presented to me along the way.

Like all good stories, to tell it properly, I must start from the beginning...

-Dan

Awakening

Lake Tahoe, California
Winter 2004/05

IN a vague kind of way, I knew how my life would go from the age of about fifteen. When finished school I would get a job and work hard for thirty or forty years until retirement. Probably I would have a wife and kids, a dog and cat. If I worked really hard, maybe even a sports car. That was the future I saw in front of me. It seemed - at the time - 'not bad'.

Growing up in a farming town in rural Australia, my family lived a middle class life. Mom and Dad were both teachers, and our family friends were either white-collar office types, or hard working salt-of-the-earth farmers. "A fair day's pay for a fair day's work" was a common slogan in Australia at the time, and everybody believed it to their very core. Working hard for life was basically a religion followed by everyone. Working full time was the goal of life.

After high school there was no question about going to University. It was simply *what you do*. So I did, and I really enjoyed it. By the end of my fifth and final year of Engineering I was exhausted - utterly fed up with eighteen straight years of schooling. My University held a job fair, where all the big employers like IBM and Oracle were scouting for talent. Too burned-out to do any schmoozing, I wandered around in a daze until I saw a huge sign:

SNOWBOARDING IN THE USA

Immediately I sensed the guy at the booth was different than everyone else in the room. And I don't just mean his long hair, jeans and skater shoes. His eyes, his smile, even the way he talked so enthusiastically with his hands - he seemed more alive than everyone else. Actually, everyone else was a zombie next to this guy. I was hooked, and as you might imagine, his was the only application I filled in that day.

Three long months later, I skip my graduation and fly to Lake Tahoe in California. On the plane I sit next to Dave, a New Zealander working as a ski patroller in Colorado. He works the winter in New Zealand, has a month or so somewhere tropical, then heads to Colorado for another winter. Back to back winters for ten straight years, and clearly loving it. Dave makes even the guy at the job fair look like a zombie, and his smile and laughter are contagious. Soon other passengers are milling about our seats to hear his stories, attempting to soak up some of whatever he has.
"Dan, after this your life will never be the same," Dave assures me with a massive grin.

I have signed up to live and work at Kirkwood Mountain Ski Resort, just outside Lake Tahoe in California. Kirkwood has on-mountain staff accommodation, and I'm randomly assigned to an apartment, already full of Americans for the season. I share a bedroom with Jeff from Oregon, who is the same age as me and has been working random jobs - mostly at ski resorts - since finishing high school. At Kirkwood he is a chef in a restaurant, which he assures me is a piece of cake, and more importantly, has good perks. Our room joins onto a communal kitchen/living area with three other bedrooms, each with two people. Ty and Ryan (Bird) are from nearby Stockton, and have a laid-back California vibe going on. Ty is a snowboard instructor and Bird works in the rental shop. Immediately I feel welcome, with Jeff and crew showing me around and captivating me with endless stories of fun in the snow over a couple of beers that first night. When I tell them I don't have a snowboard and badly want to learn, Bird immediately lends me his spare board. Ty assures I will pick it up quickly and he will teach me everything he knows.

"Have fun, it's a blast!" is all Bird says about lending me $500 worth of gear.

My job on the mountain is 'liftie' - running the massive chair-lifts that shuttle people up the mountain. Most mornings it involves shovelling huge amounts of new snow before physically slowing each chair by hand so it does not hit people in the legs. I soon realize liftie is the lowest ranking job on the mountain, and we're not seen as the brightest bunch. Amazingly, lifties take this in stride, and are actually proud of this reputation. I think they secretly love every second outside in the mountain air, rather than being cooped up in a kitchen or retail store, a fate suffered by many of our friends on the mountain.

My boss Leah is small in stature and big on personality. There are over one hundred and twenty rowdy lifties running this massive resort, and Leah whips them into shape with her quick comments and willingness to jump in and work harder than everyone else. After almost a decade on the mountain, it's clear Leah loves the everyday chaos of mountain operations.

Soon Brandon arrives from another resort and moves into our little apartment - the resort he has come from has had zero snowfall this year, which does not meet Brandon's needs for the winter one little bit. He takes being really alive to a whole new level. A few years older than me, Brandon went to university and had a 9-5 job before realizing that was not the life for him, and I can tell we have a lot in common. Now living out of his motor home affectionately named Sunshine, he skis in the winter and surfs in Southern California in the summer. Sometimes he works at ski resorts, sometimes he is a lifeguard in California. His energy is infectious, and he quickly joins our group of misfits looking for fun. He skis instead of snowboarding, though nobody cares at all. Everyone is just stoked he is having the time of his life.

Over the coming weeks I hang out with these guys whenever I'm not working, learning to snowboard as quickly as possible. Usually I cartwheel down the mountain before scrambling to the chairlift as fast as I possibly can, worried about being left behind. I arrive puffing and drenched in sweat, while the guys patiently wait for me. On the chairlift I listen carefully as snowboarding wisdom is shared, before the whole scenario repeats. Most days we don't even stop for lunch - we're having too much fun and simply forget.

At work I chat casually to guests getting on my chairlift. Soon I make it my goal to get a laugh from people in the fifteen seconds I have before the chair whisks them away. One of the lifts I work regularly has a couple of missing chairs - maintenance probably took them off years ago. Everyone expects the chairs to be spaced at regular intervals, and I soon develop a gag that never fails. Guests shuffle forward to get on, and are shocked when there is no chair where there should be one. I also act shocked, and ask them to look down as they are going up to see where the chair has fallen off. After a quick flash of fear, they assume I must be joking just as the next chair comes around, and laugh nervously as they are whisked off their feet and into the air.

First wake up

The first couple of times it happens, I'm really unsure.
"C'mon, it will be a riot," Jeff and Ty assure me.
They explain there is a full moon tonight, and they are hiking
to the snowboard park to ride the jumps and rails by moonlight.
They will ride through the park, then hike back up and do it
all over again, probably until the wee hours of the morning.

For twenty minutes I think of a long list of reasons not to go.
I have to work in the morning. I am not a great snowboarder.
Riding in the dark will be difficult. It's cold outside. I want
to sleep. I am also terrified, though trying hard not to show
it. Really, it doesn't make any sense to do such a thing. Why
would I?
Most of me wants to say no and stay safe at home, though
another small part wants to say yes to see what this is all
about.

The walk up is actually relaxing and peaceful, and we stop
often to gaze at the stars. Nobody is in a rush, so we take
our time, savoring every minute of the cool night air. At
the top, everyone is laughing and joking as we strap on our
snowboards, while I can't stop my legs from shaking. The
jumps are almost all too big for me, and I barely touch a single
rail, falling repeatedly. Even still, everyone smiles and offers
huge encouragement every time I try.
"You'll get it Danno."
"I wasn't that good after only a few weeks."
"Almost man, almost!"

Amazingly, even though I'm failing miserably, I don't feel like
a failure - actually, I feel great. Somehow, I am having a lot
of fun snowboarding badly.
Not only do these guys really know how to have a good time,
they are experts at making others have a great time too.

Almost falling asleep at work the next day, I think about how
much fun I had, and how close I came to saying no because of

all the silly reasons I thought up beforehand. Of course, they all turned out to be complete nonsense.

I make a promise to myself - I will always say yes to whatever adventure the guys have going, no matter how scared or hesitant I feel.

Second wake up

A month later I know my snowboarding has progressed when I'm the first of the crew to arrive at the chairlift. Everyone grins like mad and looks surprised when they see me waiting for them. Now I feel like part of the team, like I really belong. To keep me in check the guys take me to a run with a notorious cliff drop, assuring me I'll be fine.

I don't get any points for style as I scoot over the four foot drop, and I can't believe my eyes when Jeff throws a front flip off the cliff right next to me, landing in the deep powder and racing past like it's nothing.
These guys know how to live!

The mountain behind our apartment is part of the ski resort, though there is no chairlift to access it. To ride the untouched powder, guests pay one hundred dollars per run to be driven to the top in a snow cat, an elitist thing to do. Of course none of us has that kind of money, but we all want to ride the powder. Being so close to our house, the powder practically calls to us in our sleep, causing the guys to come up with their own version of exclusive snowboarding.
When I hear their plan, I almost say no before I stick to my promise and say yes.

We get up at 4am - well before dawn - and put on snowshoes Bird borrowed from the mountain rental shop. Without a backpack capable of holding my snowboard I simply carry it in my hands as we skip out the door into the cool night air. The hike is mostly straight up and takes the best part of three hours. The thin air at 10,000 feet causes me to puff hard the whole time, though again the hike is supremely peaceful. Somehow it just feels right to be out working so hard in the mountains. We all stare in awe as a spectacular sunrise comes and goes, and in the distance we hear ski patrol throwing explosive charges. The massive booms echo endlessly off the mountains that surround our tiny village, now far below.

At the top it's all smiles and high fives, and we linger as long as possible, not wanting the whole experience to come to an end. I take a conservative line with no rocks or cliffs, and it's easily the best powder snowboarding of my life. Before this I had no idea what real powder felt like on a snowboard - it's a completely different sport. The sense of floating, the silence, the flow. And the speed. I can't get enough of the speed.

We ride right to our backdoor, and again all slap high-fives as we race to grab gear and rush to our respective jobs. I'm a couple of minutes late and when I tell Leah I was out snow-boarding she grins like mad and shakes her head.
"Jump on a snowmobile!" she calls as I rush to my chairlift.

Working the chairlift that day I can see my squiggly line down the adjacent mountain, and I can't wipe the huge smile off my face. When a couple of people ask and I point out what I did that morning, they slap me hard on the back. "Dude, that's awesome!"

I quickly forget about my aching legs.

Third wake up

One night I go to bed early, exhausted from a day of shovelling heavy spring snow. When the guys burst in hopping with excitement, I only want to go back to sleep.

"Danno, get up right now! There is a bear outside."
"Shut up, there is not. Let me sleep. You guys are nuts."
"Danno, seriously, get your ass out of bed and check this out!!"

Eventually they drag me over to the window and I'm awestruck to see a real life bear wandering around the parking lot. I have never seen a bear before. They explain it's a grizzly, and it's huge. After I take a few photos from the window we realize that won't do at all, so Brandon and I head outside to get a closer look. The bear is occupied trying to get into a dumpster full of tasty trash, so we sneak closer and closer, using parked cars as shelter. My heart is racing and feels like it will explode from my chest as I stick my head up to snap photos. I'm certain the bear turns it's head in my direction when the flash goes off, so I turn tail and bolt back inside faster than I have ever run on snow.

When I race through the door everyone is rolling around laughing hysterically - they saw the whole thing.
The bear has not moved and didn't so much as glance in my direction.

Ψ   Ψ   Ψ

My winter at Kirkwood continues for five months, always living a life I had never dreamed possible. Every day is a grand new adventure, and I love every second.

When the snow finally melts after a record-setting season, Brandon and I hit the road in Sunshine, surfing the California coast for a month. It's a fitting end to six months of fun in the USA.
I make the long trek back to Australia and can't stop thinking about The Kirkwood Crew. None of them has much money, but they're happier than anyone I have ever met.
How do they do that?
I have to know.

Growing up in small-town Australia I thought going to work for life was the only path to happiness. I thought if I worked hard and earned a good wage I would be guaranteed a happy life. Not only did The Kirkwood Crew teach me a whole new way of being happy - without lots of money - they also taught me a whole new level of happiness I had no idea existed.

Somehow in all the years of school, lessons and studying, I had missed the classes about having fun. I missed the lessons about living right now. And I missed all the notes about how to really be alive. Luckily, these guys came along at just the right time in my life and gave me the education I had missed.

I will spend the rest of my life living the lessons I learned that winter in California.

Setting Out

Calgary, Alberta, Canada
June 2009

A FTER almost a year back in Australia, I return to North America to work at kids summer camps and ski resorts across the USA and Canada. At one resort, I stumble across a copy of *Long Way Round*[1] - Ewan McGregor and Charley Boorman's tale of their motorbike ride around the world from London to New York City. Soon I am completely engrossed and can't stop reading for two days and nights. It's one of the best books I have ever read. Ewan and Charlie journey through countries I never dreamed possible, trying new food and learning new languages. For months on end they see new places, meet new characters and set up their tents wherever they can find a quiet place. To me, this is real adventure.

---

[1] *Long Way Round: Chasing Shadows Across the World*
Ewan McGregor and Charley Boorman, 2004

I soon realize, however, this is not an achievable adventure for an ordinary guy like me. Ewan is an international superstar, and their journey cost millions of dollars and required sponsorships, support vehicles, border helpers and years of planning and logistics. The list of hurdles is endless. When I finish reading, I am left with one powerful thought:
"Too bad I can never do something like that."

Ψ   Ψ   Ψ

Completely out of money and backed into a corner, I suck it up and get an Engineering job in Calgary. It's great to rent a room, have stable friends, go the gym and cook healthy food after years of transient living. My brother Mike soon follows me to Canada, and in the winter I often make weekend visits to the Rockies so we can snowboard together. During one visit Mike hands me a book that forever changes my life.

In *Jupiter's Travels*[2], Ted Simon details his four year motorbike adventure around the world. From London to Cape Town through Africa, Rio De Janeiro to Vancouver in the Americas, around Australia and finally from South East Asia back to London through the heart of Central Asia, Ted really does ride around the entire world. While similar to Ewan and Charley's book, the life-changing part for me is the realization that Ted was a completely average guy who set out to live a dream.

Ted had never ridden a motorbike and didn't have a license. He had a tiny savings account, no sponsors and zero experience with an adventure so big. Ted was an average guy. One day he simply made the decision to do something unbelievably big.

The more I think about it, the more I realize I'm an average guy dreaming of doing something unbelievably big. I can't stop thinking how similar to Ted I am. It hits me like a ton of bricks - the only thing stopping me is deciding to go.

---

[2] *Jupiter's Travels: Four Years Around the World on a Triumph*
Ted Simon, 1979

With my days occupied at work, and my savings account slowly creeping up, I start daydreaming about where I want to go. Calgary is a fine place to live, though I sense I don't fit. Everyone around me is buying expensive cars and new clothes while I focus on the bottom line of my savings account - I walk to work and go to the bar wearing my old snowboarding jacket patched with duct tape.

Ψ   Ψ   Ψ

As the months roll by, my dreams slowly develop into a concrete plan. At Kirkwood, Jeff filled my head with stories of Alaskan adventure, awakening the fascination I felt since reading Jack London's epic *White Fang*[3] and *The Call of The Wild*[4] as a young boy. Talking about my vague idea of quitting my job and driving North to Alaska for the summer, a friend suggests an extension. After Alaska I should continue South to Mexico, he says. The beaches are amazing, tacos are cheap and delicious, and it's not difficult to drive your own car.

I have previously been to *Tijuana* from San Diego and absolutely loved it, so Mexico sounds like a great idea. In the midst of a brutal Calgary winter a few months on the beach would be paradise on earth. When I buy a map of Mexico, all of Central America stretches to the South. After staring at the map for an hour, I rush out to buy another map - South America. After another hour of staring I can't wipe the smile off my face as I connect the dots and start dreaming really, really big.

Ψ   Ψ   Ψ

For seven months my room is plastered with maps of North, Central and South America, and huge sheets of paper where I write lists of everything I need to organize, bring and plan to make the journey a reality. I have a list of Jeep work, a list of

---

[3] *White Fang* - Jack London, 1906
[4] *The Call Of The Wild* - Jack London, 1903

medial supplies to bring, a list of spare parts and tools I need and at one point, even a list of lists somehow grows. Every morning I wake staring at the maps, and every night I go to sleep with them in my dreams. I have a huge amount of work to do to and stuff to organize, so I aim to check one item off each day. With this approach the planning and preparation does not feel overwhelming, and the whole journey starts off feeling achievable.

After years of camping and hiking in the Rockies with a minimum of equipment, I'm confident the gear I already own will see me through. My two-man tent and small alcohol stove are well-loved, and both still function perfectly. Although I want to, I know deep down I don't need to buy anything new or fancy like a roof top tent, fridge, or winch for the Jeep. I plan to hit the road with a minimum of savings, which means the choice comes down to working longer to pay for new gear and upgrades on the Jeep, or to hit the road as soon as possible with what I already have.
I choose to hit the road sooner, of course.

My best guess puts the total distance at 30,000 miles - including the many detours I know I will make - which I think will take roughly a year. Both of those are ballpark estimates, and as long as I can make my savings of about $10,000 USD stretch, taking more time is great. After all, this is not a vacation from my life, it is my life.

Researching the crossing from Panama to Colombia indicates that it could turn into a logistical headache, and I find it comforting to view Panama as a possible end point. If I really dislike what I'm doing, or it's too difficult, or I feel unsafe, I can sell the Jeep in Panama and do something else with my life. I find it easier not to look at the immense task as a whole, instead only to look a few days or weeks ahead. When people tell me about Peru, I immediately zone out and try not to listen - I don't want to get overwhelmed thinking about driving my Jeep to Peru.

I mean, that's crazy!
I can't do that.

I just plan to drive North to Alaska and then South to Mexico.
After that, I will see how I feel.

Ψ   Ψ   Ψ

The months fly by, and even after counting down the last one
hundred days, I'm shocked when it is time to give notice at
work and move out. Selling and giving away stuff feels great,
and I do that repeatedly until everything I own fits comfortably
in the Jeep.
I planned and dreamed and planned for so long, leaving Calgary
turns out to be anti-climactic.

Of course, thinking about going is much harder than actually
doing it. After a small goodbye party with a few friends, I get
up one morning, get in the Jeep and start driving North.

And just like that, a 40,000 mile road-trip is underway.

The date is June 16, 2009.

The Magic Bus

Mount McKinley Area, Alaska
July 2009

T HE first time I saw *Into the Wild*[5] I was deeply affected.
Soon after I devoured the John Krakauer book[6] of the
same name, loving every page. Into The Wild tells the story
of Chris McCandless, who, after graduating university, set off
to travel the United States. Chris wanted to live mindfully
and purposefully, instead of just going to work every day with
little conscious thought. Like me, he strongly believed in the
'Less is More' approach, to the point of reducing his worldly
possessions into a single backpack. Chris met all kinds of
friendly characters as he made his way around the US, mostly
by hitchhiking. Also like me, his dream destination was Alaska.

Chris lived alone in the pristine Alaskan wilderness for many

---

[5] *Into The Wild* - directed by Sean Penn, 2007
[6] *Into The Wild* - John Krakauer, 1997

months, hiking and exploring his heart out. Sadly, Chris eventually died alone in the Alaskan wilderness. The exact cause of death is a topic of debate, though most agree he died of starvation, possibly caused by accidentally eating a mildly toxic plant that prevented his body digesting food properly. Chris' final months were spent in an abandoned bus, and trekking to this bus has become a pilgrimage made by those who feel a connection with Chris and his story. The now famous 'Magic Bus' lies on the well known Stampede Trail, not all that far from civilization. It can be reached in a single solid day of hiking, though getting there proves harder than it sounds.

Chris' story and legacy are extremely controversial. Many people are zealous with their opinion that Chris was just a dumb, ill-prepared city boy who got in over his head, whose ignorance ultimately cost him his life. Anyone following Chris' line of thought must be just as stupid, the thinking goes. Many others, like me, feel a connection to Chris. We are trying to understand our purpose and place in the world, and feel we can learn from his attitude and approach to life. The strong connection I feel to Chris and his approach to mindful living draw me into Chris' story and to the bus where he spent his final months, deep in the Alaskan wilderness.

The Stampede Trail lies just North of Denali National Park and is fifty miles of rough, overgrown mining road that was abandoned in 1963. No bridges were ever constructed over the several rivers it crosses. Today it is primarily used by backcountry travelers on foot, bicycle and snow machine. The now infamous Fairbanks City Transit bus number 142 - aka 'The Magic Bus' - was left behind by the Yutan Construction Company during the road building to serve as a backcountry shelter for hunters, trappers and ranger patrols. Shelters like this - always unlocked - can mean the difference between life and death in chilly Alaska. Chris stumbled across the bus by accident, and decided to call it home for the spring and summer of 1992.

Ψ   Ψ   Ψ

While exploring Alaska, the idea of hiking to the bus sticks in my mind. After hours of research I decide I will at least make an attempt to reach it. Crossing the many rivers blocking the way is a problem I will have to deal with when the time comes. As luck would have it I bump into a couple of high-energy Austrian mountaineers also roaming Alaska. Thomas, and (roll the 'R') Roland are a couple of larger than life characters who are bursting with excitement about exploring the North. It's quickly clear we share many of the same values, and they also want to see about hiking to the bus. Of course it makes sense to team up, and I'm grateful for the company and their immense wilderness experience.

The Stampede Trail turns off the paved highway and begins as a regular dirt road, complete with power poles and houses. It slowly deteriorates as it passes beyond the last buildings, turning into a vast field of mud and swampy lowland, caused by the many beaver dams. Progress in our vehicles slows to a crawl, and so when we find a patch of dry ground roughly thirteen miles in, we declare camp for the night. After an evening telling stories around the fire I lie awake wondering about what challenges lay ahead.

In the morning I have butterflies in my stomach as we set out on foot. I feel a sense of freedom as I catch the last glimpse of the Jeep, knowing I'm carrying everything I need in my backpack. The first ninety minutes of hiking sees us travel on a well used quad trail before trudging through multiple small swamps. The mosquitoes are soon horrendous and ravenous. Wearing a bug net over my face brings much needed relief, and I even apply 99% DEET to my legs in an attempt to deter the swarm that surrounds us. This holds the mosquitoes at bay for less than an hour before they bite again. We play games hopping over a couple of small creek crossings, trying to keep our boots dry, though we know that is never going to last. Soon we have no choice other than to wade through

small shin-deep rivers, swamping our boots.
In the late morning we reach the bank of the Teklanika River - aka 'The Tek'.

Ultimately, The Tek was Chris' downfall. When he trekked into the bus in early spring he could easily walk through what was then a small stream. After many months he was running low on food and ready to end his time in the wilderness so Chris decided to leave the bus and return to civilization. The Tek was in late summer flood, however, and he was unable to cross on foot, forcing his hand. With no other choice, Chris returned to the bus with virtually no food, and no plan for how he could leave.

Thomas, Roland and I stand on the bank of the Tek in early July, with snow-melt runoff still high in Central Alaska. Rivers here swell significantly during the hot twenty one hours of daylight, and this summer has seen a record heat wave. The Tek in front of us is not the raging torrent actor Emile Hirsch faced in the movie, though it is obvious we will be swept off our feet and downstream if we don't take this crossing seriously. A significant number of hikers making the pilgrimage require helicopter rescue, primarily because they get into trouble crossing the Tek. In my research I discovered one hiker tragically drowned while attempting to cross at this very spot only a year earlier. Any rescue simply can't reach the river in time to help in any meaningful way.

Searching up and downstream for an hour, we struggle to find a suitable crossing point. Eventually we decide enough is enough. Thomas picks a spot and after throwing in rocks and using sticks to measure the depth, we agree it's our best chance. Tentatively, Thomas wades into the fast-flowing river.

His heavy pack is un-buckled, so he can ditch it in the water in case he gets into trouble. Tall and strong, Thomas has no major problems keeping a steady pace to the far bank. Using a stick for added balance, I follow confidently into the middle, where I falter. The rocky bottom means I have unstable footing, and the rushing water pushes harder and harder, causing me to hesitate and wobble. The glacier-melt torrent is icy cold, and when it reaches mid-thigh I lose feeling in my legs and feet, making me wobble even more.

Slow and steady eventually wins through, and I am relieved to join Thomas on the far bank, who has been anxiously watching my every move. Powerful Roland is on a mission and forges steadily across without slowing once.
"Bah, dat was easy!" he bellows in a perfect Schwarzenegger imitation. I am shaking from adrenaline and cold, and I realize this crossing would have been impossible on my own.

After a short rest and snack we search the muddy bank for signs of the now overgrown trail. Endless swampy beaver dams slow our progress, and we raise our eyebrows and scan the thick brush each time we find fresh bear prints in the mud. Thomas and Roland are active International Mountain Rescue climbers, and are therefore both fitness machines. I am quickly left in their dust only a few minutes after we find the trail. Now alone, my thoughts turn to Chris, and the sense of isolation he must have felt. I'm sure being here alone, not knowing if there is anything or anyone ahead would be almost overpowering.

I constantly yell and clap my hands into the scrubby alder while hiking the overgrown trail, my strategy to avoid startling the many bears that are evidently close by. The soundtrack from Into The Wild has become one of my all-time favourites, and I sing it aloud for continuous noise. I am elated and amazed to be hiking in Chris' footsteps. I really am hiking to the bus! The bus that Chris spent four months living in, was essentially trapped in and finally died in.
Wow. This is really heavy.

Alone with my thoughts for hours, I am startled when Bus 142 appears on the side of the trail, seemingly out of thin air. Even after many hours of deep thought, somehow I feel mentally unprepared. I pause on the edge of the clearing, attempting to take in everything around me. After dropping my pack, I again pause in the open doorway, feeling a sense of disorientation and familiarity at the same time. Though I have never been to the bus before, it feels familiar. The descriptions in the book and the re-creation used for the movie are perfectly accurate, causing a strong sense of déjá vu. Roland and Thomas lounge nearby in the afternoon sun, so I have the bus all to myself.

Riddled with bullet holes and dents, the bus is tired and sadly neglected. Most windows are smashed out, glass litters the clearing and a mountain of trash is stuffed into the bushes behind. It seems to be more rust than metal. Inside, the air is damp and thick with the smell of mold and decay. The small wood stove looks functional and would be an agreeable sight on a winter day. The mattress on the rusty springs is extremely moldy and shredded, leaving a lot to be desired. There is a lone chair up front, and an old suitcase with a few of Chris' belongings still inside.

It is customary for visitors to graffiti their name on the wall and write a message to Chris in the 'Guest Book'. The book was placed in the bus by Chris' sister Carine and author Jon Krakauer, on their first visit to the bus soon after Chris' remains were identified. Scanning through the book my hair stands on end and I feel a strange combination of calm and exhilaration.

There are hundreds, maybe even thousands of detailed messages from people all over the world who have trekked to the bus. The book is bursting with stories of how Chris' story forever changed people's lives. Through his purposeful living and courage, Chris inspired countless people to live their dreams.

One story is about hitching thousands of miles to reach the bus, while another is of a father and son who spent a week together at the bus. Many write about how beautiful and peaceful a place Chris had found. Graffiti like "Solo trek to honor Chris" and "Swept downstream by Tek - worth it" make me grin from ear to ear. The more I read, the clearer it becomes how much of an inspiration Chris has been to so many people. Like me, they were drawn to the bus and eventually made the trek to soak in the atmosphere and say thanks to Chris.

My message in the Guest Book captures my feelings:

> *Chris,*
> *You have inspired more people than you will ever know, including me. Your passion, courage and determination gave me the strength to believe I really can make my dreams come true. And here I am, in Alaska, having been to the Arctic Ocean, on my way to South America.*
> *Thank you Chris.*

Many visitors have written quotes on the bus from Chris' favourite authors - Jack London and Henry Thoreau - though I can't find any writing from Chris himself. It seems to have all faded over the almost two decades since Chris spent his summer in the bus.

We camp in the clearing beside the bus, huddling close to a smouldering campfire in an attempt to drive off the relentless mosquitoes. I spend many quiet hours both inside the bus and on the shores of the nearby stream, contemplating the isolation and peacefulness I would feel out here, all alone. The Alaskan wilderness is immense, and I feel dwarfed by the vastness around me, despite my nearby friends. I can only guess how intense the experience must have been for Chris, alone for many months.

Before making the pilgrimage, I assumed the bus would be a sombre place. After all, Chris did actually die here. As it turns out, the opposite is true. With all the inspiring messages and stories shared in the bus, there is an unmistakable feeling of excitement and happiness, with not a hint of sadness. The people that trek to the bus understand that Chris was living his life exactly how he wanted to - he made a conscious choice to live purposefully. Although it ultimately cost him his life, it is not sad because Chris lived exactly how he wanted.

I think it's possible Chris lived more in those years than many people live in their entire lives.

Of all the lessons I can learn from Chris, I want to remember this one most of all. Not to live on autopilot, unsure of meaning or place, but to always live my life consciously and with purpose.

Where the Icebergs Roam

Valdez, Alaska
July 2009

C ONSCIOUSLY or not, while roaming the North I have been searching for a truly Alaskan experience. Something unique to Alaska. Something that will leave an impression I will never forget.
Alaska is epic, and I want to do something epic.

Infamous Valdez lies at the Southern end of the mighty Alaska Pipeline and sits in a stunning bay that is Alaska's most Northerly ice-free port year round. Originally a tiny fishing town, it is the textbook definition of 'coastal Alaska fishing village'. Surrounded by glacier-capped peaks which feel close enough to reach out and touch, the harbor is breathtaking. Sleepy during the day, the small docks become a hive of activity each afternoon as the many fishermen return with their catch. Walking the length of main street only takes five minutes, and both times I pause to look at photos in the two kayak guiding outfits. There are numerous trips on offer - from a few hours to a few days - and all look otherwordly. Unfortunately, all trips are over a hundred dollars, and I'm already conscious of my quickly diminishing savings.

It happens to be my Mom's birthday, so I call from the payphone at the Harbour Master's, right in the thick of the fishermen arriving for the afternoon. After a huge catch up and me raving about adventures in Alaska, I explain the kayak trip, and my money worries.

"Dan," my Mom says, "this is your life, right now."
"Today."
"You have to enjoy every minute. Too soon you will be back at work, but here and now you can have this amazing experience. There will always be more money to earn, so don't worry about it."

With this new perspective I practically run to sign up for a kayaking trip to the Colombia glacier, almost bouncing off the pavement in excitement. Moms always know the right thing to say.

Eight the next morning can not come soon enough, and in my excitement I arrive almost forty minutes early. Soon a scruffy guy arrives and introduces himself as Jay, our guide for the day. Jay is from Colorado, with long hair and a smile that lights up his entire face. Jay comes to Alaska every summer for guiding and loves to chat.
"The pay stinks, but my office ROCKS!"

Jay has a relaxed attitude and I can tell immediately we're going to get on great. He reminds me of myself, when I'm not being an office drone. Along with three other paddlers, we catch a water taxi for the ninety minute ride to Columbia glacier.

$$\Psi \quad \Psi \quad \Psi$$

We pass Bligh Reef, which made global headlines in 1989 for all the wrong reasons. The *Exxon Valdez* ran aground here, spewing crude oil into the pristine waters of Prince William Sound. When all was said and done, a total of eleven million gallons poured into the water. There are still mixed reports about the on-going impacts of the spill, now two decades ago. Studies funded by the oil companies find everything A-OK, while studies funded by other interests find lasting severe impacts. Digging in the beach sand on any nearby island it's easy to strike thick black oil, Jay says.

I'm no expert, but that doesn't sound good.

The whole incident is infamous, and of course there are many versions of what actually happened that night. Yes, the Captain really had been drinking - though officially it was his night off. He was in his cabin, not in any way commanding the ship when the incident occurred. Given the ship is his home, I think he deserves the odd night off. Amazingly, as the senior officer on board, the Captain was technically in control of the vessel - while sound asleep in his bunk.

The Third Mate was actually at the helm, and was not using the collision avoidance radar because it was broken - and had been for over a year. Exxon had not repaired it because they decided it was too expensive to run. Without the much-needed radar, the Third Mate drove the enormous tanker right into Bligh Reef. The incident was greatly exacerbated when he did not want to admit his mistake and waited hours before notifying anyone of the spill - critical hours that could have contained the oil to a much smaller area. Worse still - attempting to free the ship he reversed, un-corking the massive hole in the hull, allowing the oil to freely spew out.

Originally ordered to pay $5 billion in damages to the state of Alaska, Exxon weaseled their way out. After decades of appeals they have only paid a tiny fraction of that amount. Shockingly, Exxon actually sued the state, claiming they interfered with the clean-up operation. Exxon also lay the blame on the coast

THE ROAD CHOSE ME Vol. 1

guard, because they allowed the broken ship to sail without the radar. In their own eyes, Exxon did nothing wrong.

It blows my mind an oil company can spill eleven million gallons of crude oil into the pristine Alaska waters and then sue the state. Exxon also officially blame the sleeping captain for crashing the ship.
Talk about passing the buck.

All things considered, it was a massive screw up. Now it's obvious the town of Valdez will never again tolerate such a thing. Virtually the entire town is on alert and runs constant drills to train for the next accident. Oil will be pumped down the massive pipeline and transferred onto ships in Valdez for many decades to come, so unfortunately the next accident is really only a matter of time.

By pure luck, a few days after the Exxon Valdez started spewing oil a storm whipped up and pulled the oil away from Valdez. Miraculously, the storm spared the town from being inundated with crude. A few of the nearby fjords were also luckily spared, and the area we will paddle today was not affected.

$$\Psi \quad \Psi \quad \Psi$$

The waiting is agonizing and I'm still jumping out of my skin when we unload the water taxi, gather our gear and paddle out. I have been partnered with Faye, a gentle elderly lady visiting Alaska with her family in the other kayak. Jay puts me in the rear of our tandem kayak where I have the steering. Faye is content to sit and not paddle, and I'm perfectly happy to paddle for the two of us.

Initially we paddle close to shore, spotting wildlife along the rocky coastline. We see many bald eagles, sea otters and sea lions as we glide silently past, all of which is just the lead up to the main event.

Colombia glacier itself is so far away I can hardly see it. Winding down from the mountains, the glacier ends with a massive vertical face where the ice breaks off, leaving icebergs in the ocean - an event called calving. Tens of thousands of icebergs have calved, and are now bobbing on the gentle ocean swell directly in front of me.

As we glide closer I can hardly believe my eyes. The icebergs come in every conceivable size, shape, color and texture. Some are just grapes, others are bigger than buses. I can see every shape from perfectly round spheres to jagged chunks of jumbled ice. Some are such a shade of aqua-blue they look fake, and others are so white and frosted they look like giant snow balls, not really ice at all. They virtually all protrude much further underwater than above.

The most distinctive icebergs appear to be made mostly of dirt and rock, with almost no ice. Jay explains these are the pieces of glacier that were closest to the edges of the valley millions of years ago. Jammed against the rock with so much force, the ice tears into the rock and drags it down the mountain - a kind of accelerated super-slow motion erosion. Because these 'bergs are so dark in color, they absorb a lot more heat from the sun, causing them to melt much faster. The constant dripping of melting ice is at first eerie, and then becomes comforting and even relaxing.

Before paddling into the ice field, Jay pulls us into a group to give a safety talk about being in and around the 'bergs. While they look friendly and inviting, they are anything but, Jay explains. Bumping into them must be avoided at all costs, and whenever possible we should not get closer than about fifteen feet, he says. Because of the tides and swell, they are constantly on the move in unpredictable ways and we really don't want to get sandwiched between them. Right in the middle of his talk, an enormous chunk of ice breaks off a nearby 'berg. First we hear a shockingly loud crack, and then extremely loud crashing and smashing as it tumbles down into the water. These sounds of destruction reverberate around for several seconds, at first off all the ice and water and then inside our heads.

"Right," Jay says, "that is exactly what we're trying to avoid."

Paddling in and around the bergs is a unique blend of calm and intensity rolled into one. Sometimes we sit silently on the glassy water just listening to the dripping and far off cracking, creaking and smashing. Then other times a 'berg the size of a VW Beetle appears from nowhere and zooms past, propelled by some unseen current. Frantically, I paddle my heart out just to stay out of the way. Just as quickly as it came the excitement ends, leaving us floating silently once again.

A couple of times Jay lines up and says exactly when to 'shoot the gap' - straight lining a narrow opening between floating chunks of ice. With no other choice we must paddle closer than is safe, and simply go for it. With all the ice constantly jostling and moving in different directions, it's impossible to tell how quickly any gap might close. There is also no way to know if a gap will ever reopen to permit our escape should we need it. My adrenaline peaks every time I paddle hard to get through a quickly-closing gap - by far my favourite part of the day. When I'm extremely close to the biggest 'bergs I can study the surface in detail and see exactly how far underwater they extend. I am awed by the massive chunks of ice.

We stop for lunch on a rocky island and hike to high ground for a better view of the gigantic ice field surrounding us. The scale is impossible to comprehend, with floating ice stretching far into the distance. Closer to the glacier it's so tightly packed there is no visible water at all. From this vantage point I can finally get a good look at the calving face of the glacier. The vertical face is over four hundred feet high and nine miles away - absolutely astounding and impossible to judge as there is nothing nearby to give perspective.

The tide rises during our break and the scene has changed dramatically when we get back on the water. Icebergs that were previously as big as houses are now only small cars, while others have apparently rolled over to show a completely new size, shape and color. All the ice is moving erratically and faster than before, constantly jostled by the moving tides.

When time is up I don't want to leave - I'm so enchanted by the spectacle I could happily paddle in the ice field for days. I'm still buzzing while chatting in the water taxi - this has been one of the best experiences of my life.

Truly epic.

The West Coast Trail

Vancouver Island, British Columbia, Canada
September 2009

F OR as long as I can remember I have looked up to my big brother Mike. Trying to keep up with him has always been a great way to push my limits and inevitably hurt myself. Recently we have been pushing each other to attempt ever more ambitious adventures. While I was sitting at a desk in Calgary saving money, Mike once again raised the bar and showed me what true adventure looks like. He hiked two-thousand, two-hundred miles from Springer Mountain in Georgia to Mount Katahdin in Maine. Mike through-hiked the entire length of The Appalachian Trail over the course of five and a half months. The hike changed his life and of course he loved every second.

Since moving to Canada a few years ago, hiking The West Coast Trail - Canada's most famous trail - has been in our sights. Of course, we need to hike it together. Severe weather and other adventures have more than once forced us to shelve our plans and bide our time. Now, finally, we can make it happen.

The West Coast Trail was used by the First Nations people of the area for centuries before foreign sailing ships entered the picture. The rugged and remote coastline claimed many unsuspecting ships over the years, and so from 1888 to 1890 the government built a telegraph line and lighthouse. The hope was to save lives through better communications. Twenty-odd years later a second lighthouse was constructed, and the trail following the telegraph line was greatly improved to act as a life-saving escape route for shipwreck victims. As technology improved, shipwrecks became a thing of the past, and the trail was eventually abandoned until 1973 when it became part of the newly established Pacific Rim National Park.

Today the forty-seven mile trail is by far the most famous and popular in Canada, for very good reason. In fact the trail is often listed in the top ten world's best hiking trails. Due to the spectacular coastline, remoteness and the technicalities of the hike, visitors from all over the globe flock to this remote corner of Vancouver Island each summer.

Ψ   Ψ   Ψ

Mike and I meet North of Vancouver, just outside Whistler. We don't stop chatting and laughing as we spend a sunny afternoon throwing disc golf and catching up on our recent adventures. Mike jumps in the Jeep and together we make our way onto Vancouver Island and around to sleepy Port Renfrew, the Southern trail head.

On arrival we discover Port Renfrew brews it's own weather, mostly of the ocean-side misty and damp variety. The morning after camping near a logging road outside town, we discover the tent is soaking wet. At first confused, we realize the moisture is thick ocean fog that settles on everything, a daily occurrence we eventually take as normal.

Excited to start hiking, we amble into the Ranger Station soon after it opens planning to hit the trail immediately. Much to our surprise, the friendly Ranger says we will not be hiking today. The number of hikers per day is strictly controlled to minimize damage to the trail and campsites. Not wanting to make a pricey reservation weeks in advance, we have chosen to wing it. Now we have missed out on the quota for today, and must wait until tomorrow.

Not seeing this as a problem, we register to hit the trail first thing tomorrow morning. The fee just for hiking the trail is a steep $160 USD each, a little difficult to swallow. The Ranger explains this is to cover the cost of trail maintenance and the rescue of more than ten hikers per year that are plucked from the trail by helicopter.
This whole undertaking is beginning to sound much harder than I thought.

Crammed inside the stuffy ranger hut, we feel overwhelmed by the many hikers gearing up, about to hit the trail. We sit quietly off to the side, observing and learning what we can, while making sure we are sufficiently caffeinated for our rest day. When everyone eventually leaves, we get to chatting with the friendly Ranger who shares a couple of crazy rescue stories from just the last few days. One hiker was attacked by a swarm of wasps and another had their cooking stove explode, badly burning their face. Both events sound nasty, and we agree to do our best to avoid mishaps like these.

"I have a video here you just have to see," the Ranger says with a broad smile just as we head for the door.
Mike and I look at each other and sense something great.
"Sounds great."
"Right on."

We sit in the back room of the cozy parks office and watch a simple, low budget documentary, called *Sombrio*[7]. It tells the story of a community of squatters and surfers who lived for over thirty years at Sombrio Beach on Vancouver Island's West Coast, just South of where we are sitting. The film depicts the simple and happy lives of the people who were able to build their friendly little community from scratch and live peacefully for decades. Sadly they were forced out of their self-built homes in the late 1990's when the Juan de Fuca hiking trail was built. The new trail cut right through their homes, and so the government forced them to leave.

This eclectic collection of people had formed a functioning community in the wilderness, using little more than their wits and a respect for simplicity and their environment. Despite this, the powers-that-be decided to destroy this peaceful and happy community. No amount of appeals or protests made a difference, and eventually everyone left peacefully of their own accord, not wanting a confrontation.

Mike and I have both become disenchanted by society lately, and so the story resonates deeply with us. Neither of us particularly likes what modern consumer society has become, and we are both searching for an alternative. This is one of the reasons I set out on this journey, and also why Mike hiked in the wilderness for thousands of miles.

We find it insane to measure standard of living and happiness by how much each person consumes. To Mike and I, this is a clear example of how our industrialized society has become so disconnected from people and communities. Surely more consumption does not create more happiness. Surely there is a better path to happiness than consumption. We often discuss if the solution is to change society, or just to leave it behind.

We thoroughly enjoy Sombrio, an inspiring example of people choosing to live peacefully outside our materialistic society.

---

[7] *Sombrio: DVD* - Paul Manly, 2010

Later in the day we stroll around Port Renfrew, not doing anything in particular. Always fascinated by the ocean, we wander onto the fishing dock and immediately recognise a character from the Sombrio story - 'Rivermouth Mike'. His hand-made house was on the mouth of the river, hence the nickname.

"Hey! We just saw you in the movie Sombrio!", Mike says with a big smile.

"I am really glad to meet you," he replies with a sincerity that is so unusual we feel a bit uncomfortable. Right away we feel he is actually talking to us, not just talking to fill the space. He is communicating directly with us. Wow.

"Do you still get down to Sombrio?" I wonder aloud.

"I surf there almost every day," Rivermouth Mike replies, "more in the winter," he adds, unable to contain his infectious grin. "Nice!" we reply in unison. Neither of us can surf, though we both try every chance we get.

Rivermouth Mike continues with warm chatter about days gone by and life as it is now, keen to share with a couple of strangers from afar. Something about him makes both Mike and I want nothing more than to hang around and absorb his passion for life. His face and eyes are so alive - a blend of crazy and enlightened, I think.

Finally we drag ourselves away, both beaming and feeling lucky to have met Rivermouth Mike. We realize how fortunate we are to have met a man who lived away from this society for so many years. By forming a community and working together, he and his friends were able to live happily and comfortably, and not want for anything.

We both agree we can learn a lot from people like Rivermouth Mike.

The rest of the day is dedicated to organizing hiking gear and food, walking around town and drinking cup after cup of cheap coffee. Late in the afternoon we find a beautiful sheltered spot for the tent, right beside the beach. Watching sunset together over our free camp feels fantastic, and we agree how fortunate we are to find happiness in simple things.

Ψ   Ψ   Ψ

Early the next morning we leave the Jeep in a secure parking lot and hitch in the back of a pickup with other hikers to the trail head. Before hiking a single step we must catch a ferry across the Gordon River. While waiting for the ferry, more hikers arrive and soon we are entertained weighing our packs on a set of hanging scales on the dock.

Mike and I ring in at thirty-six and forty pounds respectively, ten pounds lighter than the next lightest pack. One young guy, about half my size, will be carrying sixty-two pounds on his back! We can't help but feel sorry for him. Long ago Mike and I learned a heavy pack makes for a happy camper, but a light pack makes for a happy hiker, and there is a lot more hiking than camping on a trail like this.

Everyone appears a little nervous and even intimidated by the hike, and for some reason they assume Mike and I are experts. Someone later explains it's our bushy beards and tattered clothes that make us look seasoned. Many are keen to talk about how long we estimate the hike will take, assuming we will set a blistering pace. They are taken aback when we shrug our shoulders and grin our usual answer to such questions: "As long as it takes."

After the short ferry ride, we pose together for a customary 'start' photo before skipping into the dense coastal forest. Content at my own pace, Mike quickly disappears. After only five minutes, a thick fog descends, and I soon feel isolated among the towering trees. I have been told repeatedly the first six miles are the hardest of the entire trail, and actually causes many people to quit in the first hours. The majority of hikers prefer to start at the other end and cover this section on their last day, because it will be easier when their packs are lighter. Personally, I prefer to tackle it while I'm eager and fresh.

Soon I'm in the thick of it; mud, tree roots, uphill, downhill, bridges and ladders. I quickly discover everything is very, very slippery. This coastline has seen one of the driest summers on record so far, so I can only imagine the mud in a wet year. Saying a cheery hello to those hiking in the opposite direction, I notice how exhausted and dirty everyone is. Most can barely nod a reply to my greeting, and all are dragging their feet badly, tripping over every log and root. I also notice everyone stinks - and not just of campfire.

I revel in the feeling that everything I need for the next week is on my back. I have a minimum of stuff in the Jeep, though even still it can sometimes feel like a burden. Dealing with maintenance, parking and buying gas can occasionally feel like the focus of my life. Now, walking through the coastal forest, I genuinely have the absolute minimum of stuff. It's a fantastic feeling to carry it all on my back.

I catch up with Mike after a couple of hours, stretched out like a lizard on a sunny log. He insists he has been studying the trail map, though I wonder how he was able to do that with his eyes closed. Studying the map together, we're excited to see a choice ahead. In many places we can choose to hike inland in the dense forest, or to hike along the many beaches. We have been told the forest is always dark, wet and muddy where the massive trees block any chance of a view. On the other hand, the beaches are wide open, often have a nice breeze, and offer spectacular views. It's an easy choice to climb down a string of wooden ladders to Thrasher Cove on the beach, where we declare a lunch stop.

Wanting to stay on the beach as much as possible, we look further and further ahead. Hiking around Owen Point requires the tides to be just right, so we wait a couple of hours in the amazing sunshine, trying to sink into the hike. After carefully studying the tide chart provided with the trail map, we move off exactly as the tide begins to turn. Scrambling around the point requires a lot of tricky rock-hopping and we are soon laughing and smiling as we reminisce about doing exactly this as kids on our annual family camping trips to the beach in Australia.

At Owen Point we stumble into colorful rock caves right at water level, and immediately explore. While poking around we discover an alternate trail that has us use ropes to climb and descend vertical rock, allowing us to avoid the still too-high tide.

We continue on the beach as long as possible, before we are eventually forced inland for the final stretch of the day. Crossing a river requires the use of our first cable car, the highlight of the day. We climb into the tiny carriage one at a time with our packs, before pulling ourselves across hand over hand. When one person arrives, the car is pulled back and the process repeated. Playing around like children, we have great fun. After an easy seven and half miles for our first day, we wander into Camper Bay, home for the night.

The number of people milling about is staggering. I find it hard to believe there can be so many when numbers are restricted per day. I count fourteen tents scattered around when we arrive, with more popping up by the minute. We are happy to bump into people we recognise from the ferry this morning, including the young guy carrying the monster sixty-two pound pack. They chose to hike inland for the entire day, and soon confirm the muddy and slippery tree roots really are endless. While we were lounging on the beach waiting for the tides, they were on an endless mud-slog. They're all exhausted and covered from head to toe in mud, in direct contrast to our relatively clean clothes and energetic steps that garner stares of disbelief.

We move a hundred yards towards the ocean to find a great secluded place for our tent. After setting up we wander to the main area to chit-chat, and are dismayed to watch ravens carry off our entire supply of granola, which I left sitting on my pack. We soon laugh and wonder how many people have unintentionally fed those ravens.

When the sun hits the horizon a fire is lit, slowly drawing everyone in. Small conversations erupt all around, and I'm content to sit and listen to all the various trail stories. Almost immediately I am struck by the juxtaposition between the hikers just starting, and those almost finished. It seems everyone starting is missing their creature comforts, while those nearly finished are dreading going back to 'The Real World'. Clearly, they want to stay in the woods much longer.

I begin to wonder if everyone has a little Rivermouth Mike inside - maybe it just takes time in the wilderness to discover.

$$\Psi \quad \Psi \quad \Psi$$

In the morning we have an inland stretch, slogging through the deep mud, causing us to drag our feet. Morale improves at an impressive vertical drop of six giant ladders, descending a deep valley. Five yards across the valley floor, six more equally impressive ladders climb straight back up.
Climbing vertically with my heavy pack is unnerving - the weight tries to pull me backwards off the ladder, a feeling I don't like one bit.

Looking forward to the only river crossing on the trail, we are disappointed the river is barely more than a trickle that we easily hop over.

Later in the afternoon, we walk along beach and rock-shelf to finish ten miles for the day. After making camp at Carmanah Creek, we quickly throw everything in the tent before exploring along the creek. Without my heavy pack I feel like an explorer on the moon, virtually leaving the ground with every step. I'm amused to watch ravens gather at the tent, clearly searching for any food left outside.

A local in Port Renfrew told us about the world's largest sitka spruce tree, The Carmanah Giant. Amazingly, this monster tree lies only half a mile up the creek from the busy campsite. Rock-hopping with tired legs is hilarious and we both inevitably get a boot wet in the shallow water, laughing the whole time. Worried about passing the monster tree, I wonder aloud if we will be able to spot it from the creek. The second we do, I stop wondering. The trunk is at least five times broader than any nearby tree - over thirty-three feet across. Even more impressive is the height - three hundred and twelve feet. The base of this giant is at creek level, and still it easily towers over every other tree - even those growing from the top of the valley.

Camp is eerily deserted when we return from our little side trek, as everyone has hiked along the beach to the First Nations Reservation where burgers and cold beer are for sale. Apparently, the temptation is too great. Many hikers have mentioned it - a real highlight, they say. Nobody seems to care they cost $25 USD.

Instead of walking there, we dig 'seats' into the beach sand and lay down to relax. Soon Mike spots a couple of whales breaching in the calm bay, and we sit captivated while the sun slowly sets. We boil water and thoroughly enjoy our meal of de-hydrated food and powdered mash potatoes. It occurs to us we are not drawn to the burgers and beer because we don't feel like we are sacrificing, or missing out on anything by being here in the wilderness.
Sitting in the cool beach sand, watching whales at sunset and eating de-hydrated food is exactly where we want to be.

$$\Psi \quad \Psi \quad \Psi$$

Early the next morning, while the tide is low, we attempt to hike around the point below the Carmanah Lighthouse. We get chatting to the lighthouse keeper who tells us most people turn back from the slippery seaweed-covered cliff below. Of course, now we see that path as a challenge. With Mike in front we move quickly, though at one point we both stop to watch at least ten waves, trying to guess our chances of making it. We both agree we will be fine, with wet boots the worst case scenario. There are not nearly enough dry rocks, and so we attempt to rock climb sideways to get around. Climbing with a heavy pack turns out to be a lot more strenuous than I thought. Seeing the inevitable, I don't move a muscle while my foot is on a low rock. I am perfectly happy with a soaked boot instead of scrambling and risking a fall into the churning waters below.

As the day winds on we continue along the beach and rock-shelf before finally moving inland for the afternoon. We are both shocked by the disrepair of the boardwalks - broken and rotting boards outnumber whole ones. Boardwalks fifty and one hundred yards long are slanted in all directions and move dangerously under our weight. Hundreds of sharp rusty nails poke out, and everything is incredibly slippery. We have never seen a trail in such decay and agree it would be much safer to remove the rotting boardwalks and slog through the knee deep mud.
It is becoming crystal clear why so many rescues are needed on this trail.

When we arrive at the Nitnat Narrows Ferry we see other hikers eating salmon and crab while drinking expensive beer. The First Nations People have again found their captive audience and are taking full advantage.

The Nitnat Narrows is a huge tidal inlet that feeds a monster lake far inland. Because the water can't move in and out as fast as the tides, there are extremely strong and dangerous currents as the surging water lags behind the tides. The narrows are only a hundred yards across, though the water boils ominously. A rumor persists about a guy swimming during the slack tide, though it's not something we're about to try, opting to cruise across in the powerful ferry instead.

The official Trail Map has one interesting bullet point we discuss at length:

- Assume all surfaces are slippery

We conclude the word 'assume' can be removed after we both slip and fall repeatedly. My best effort comes while hiking a rock shelf between the beach and waves. The rock is under an inch of water and is coated with thick green moss and slime.

After a few minor slips and stumbles, I finally completely loose my footing, doing my best impression of slipping on a banana peel. My legs fly up in front of me as I flail my arms in an attempt to maintain balance before I land hard on my backside and pack on the wet rocks. I get a good soaking, and of course a big dent in my pride. Mike bursts out laughing, and we are both quickly in hysterics, which last a long time.
When I finally pick myself up I have to smile that Mike's first reaction was to burst out laughing, then ask if I am injured.

We continue inland to Tsusiat Falls, our campsite for the night after thirteen miles. Photos show spectacular falls during a high rainfall year, though we find only a small trickle sliding down some rocks. Mike announces he has a cold and puts himself to bed the minute I finish setting up the tent. He will not even get out of bed to eat dinner - though I eventually convince him and he is happier for it.

$$\Psi \quad \Psi \quad \Psi$$

It rains hard overnight and continues into the morning. We are lucky to pack-up the tent in a brief respite, keeping our gear dry. After only an hour on the trail, the weather clears and we are treated to another warm, sunny day. With only eight miles to hike, we thoroughly enjoy ourselves - relaxing into the hiking routines and lounging around, taking our time at lunch. Sitting around the campfire at Michigan Creek that night, all of us Northbound hikers are in high spirits - we have only one short day to finish.

For our fifth and final day we wake to heavy rain, and deep puddles surround the tent. We agree it would not be an authentic West Coast Trail Experience^{TM} without solid rain. In fact, we're getting off easily, and we know it. By the time we cook breakfast and pack up, everything is soaked through. The knowledge we have only eight miles to finish gets us moving.

The only trail is inland, through dense forest, mud and extremely slippery tree roots. The rain makes everything worse than ever, and a creek flows along the trail for most of the day. We ponder how different the hike would be if it had rained for five days. After only a couple of hours we're covered head to toe in mud and our worn-out rain jackets begin to let water in. Luckily, we don't care.

As we near the end we instinctively slow down, trying to lengthen the experience. Passing hikers just starting in the opposite direction is jarring. They are immaculately clean, and even smell nice. Is that makeup I see?

I smile from ear to ear as it occurs to me I am now that guy. I am covered from head to toe in mud and I stink of campfire!

$$\Psi \quad \Psi \quad \Psi$$

Just like Rivermouth Mike and his friends who formed a community at Sombrio, we can learn a lot when there are no material distractions. Chatting to other hikers, it was obvious how hesitant everyone was to head into the wilderness - they were afraid to leave their secure and comfortable lives. By the end of the trail the same people turned a complete circle and were reluctant to return to their 'normal' lives, so enjoyable was their time in the wilderness. Even the guy with the super-heavy pack has a smile plastered on his face, extremely happy with his achievement.

Time in the wilderness away from society must be good for us.

I vow to head out as often as possible in the future.

Into Mexico

Tijuana, Mexico
November 2009

F OR the last six months, I have had the following conversation more times than I can count:

"I am driving to South America."
After a long pause, the reply is invariably always
"Wait. You're going to Mexico?"
"Yep."
"It's extremely dangerous there, you can't go."
"Many people who have been recently loved it."
"You can't go, you will get kidnapped and beheaded by the drug cartels on day one."
"When was the last time you were in Mexico?"
"Well...I have never been to Mexico. But it's extremely dangerous. Everyone knows that. You will die."
"I'll take my chances."

Given the sheer volume of people certain I will die, I would rather not cross the border alone, so I meet my friend Duke in San Diego. We became good friends years ago after striking up a conversation while sitting on the same chairlift at Kirkwood. Duke is tall and muscular, has long blond surfer hair, piecing blue eyes and is the most confident person I have ever met. Blend in he does not.

Together we drive South on I5 until the end, literally at the huge fence on the Mexican border. When the officer directing traffic sees us it becomes clear I'm in the wrong lane. With some difficulty, I traverse four lanes of moving traffic into the 'Declaration' lane, where I should have been from the start. This officer only speaks Spanish, while I speak virtually none. Hand gestures and smiles make it clear he would like to look inside the Jeep. After a cursory poke around the back he quickly loses interest.

Twice he repeats *"¿Uno?"* before I realize he is asking if we will drive on Highway One and therefore Baja California.
"Si," I reply, *"é Mazatlán."*
Going to *Mazatlán* on the mainland means I have to get myself a Tourist Visa and a Temporary Import Permit for the Jeep. Using the three words of Spanish I have been practicing for a week, I ask where to find Immigration and Customs.

We park next to the flowing traffic and find the Immigration building. The officer explains in broken English we must walk two blocks to an office that can take care of the required paperwork for the Jeep. We start walking before quickly realizing he means for us to walk through the turnstiles into downtown *Tijuana*. I have been to *Tijuana* before on day trips on foot, giving me a decent feel for the place. Walking in now is not something I am particularly excited about, especially while the Jeep sits in the busy border area and I am carrying all my important paperwork.

We decide to scrap the whole paperwork-at-the-border plan, delaying it until we reach the Southern tip of Baja California.

I am immediately happier back in the Jeep - I always feel at home behind the wheel. While searching for the winding roads and confusing turns leaving *Tijuana* I'm extremely thankful to have a navigator. We are on the lookout for signs to *Ensenada* and highway 1D, which always appear the instant before we must exit.

I can't take my eyes off the busy road for long, though when I do memories come flooding back. I see decrepit buildings all around, garbage and filth coat every surface possible and desolate people stare blank-eyed, as if in a trance. With no air conditioning we have the windows down and so the smells also come in full force. First a rotting dead animal, then wave after wave of rotting fish and finally the most powerful sewage stench I have ever experienced. All of this is combined with low-hanging smoke from mountains of burning trash, and thick black smoke belching from trucks. The air actually feels thick - not only does it smell awful, I can taste it too. In only five minutes we have quite literally driven into a different world from sunny San Diego.
We both fall silent, trying to digest our new surroundings.

In all the warnings of rape, kidnap and murder, I have consistently been warned the major problem areas in Mexico are alongside the border. It has always been my plan to drive as far South as possible on the first day in Mexico. I hope to put as much distance as possible between us and the border. Moving through toll booths we pay $2 USD multiple times on our way to *Ensenada*, which turns out to be a huge city. Even after only a couple of hours in Mexico it's strange to see a row of box stores complete with a Walmart Supercenter, McDonalds, Burger King, Scotia Bank and Home Depot. When I squint my eyes, I could easily be in a strange part of the US or Canada. With that thought in the front of my mind a few blocks later, the shopping district comes to an abrupt end and my vision is again filled with trash, smoke and poverty.

I have also been warned repeatedly about the crazy drivers

and roads throughout Latin America. Roads are not a place for cars to move swiftly and safely - as you might think - but are more commonly used for every other purpose imaginable, and therefore I must always drive accordingly. In only the first few hours I encounter the following road hazards.

At the time, I was completely clueless these would become daily occurrences for the next eighteen months of my life.

- Pot holes the size of the Jeep tires.
- Severe speed bumps, without any warning signs. (called *Topes* in Mexico)
- Construction and highway surfaces so bad they require first gear in the Jeep.
- Beasts of burden pulling carts on the road - including donkeys painted to look like zebras.
- Kids playing on the road, complete with volleyball nets and soccer goal posts across the road.
- Food being dried on huge tarps directly on the road.
- Broken down vehicles in the middle of the driving lane, often with men working around the vehicle.
- Huge boulders left behind after being used to stop broken-down vehicles rolling.
- Police and Military roadblocks (Duke's favourite).

The Police and Military in Mexico evidently do not mess around - about every fifteen miles we pass through a heavily fortified roadblock, manned by stern men in full combat gear. All are wearing riot helmets, bullet proof vests and hold assault rifles at the ready. Conversation with the officers is difficult and they seem more amused by us than anything else. At each roadblock we are quickly waved through with little interest. It is obvious we are tourists, which these men are accustomed to and they don't bother to search the Jeep, apparently not interested in whatever is going South.

A few hours later we stop at a small bank in a nondescript town. The ATM has an English option, and withdrawing money is no problem, something I had been wondering about. Duke's Spanish is passable, so we order lunch from a small roadside shack - a delicious omelet with *chorizo* for a couple of dollars each.

Now feeling more confident and at ease with our surroundings, we stop to buy gas at a Pemex station, the government owned gas stations all across Mexico. I come to learn they are often brand new, clean and friendly. When I say *"mas, mas"* (more, more) the smiling attendant teaches me how to say 'full' in Spanish - *lleno*. He is clearly happy to meet us and although we can not converse, many smiles and handshakes get the message across.

Without being fully aware of it, my life in Latin America has just begun.

Baja to Mainland Mexico

Baja California, Mexico
November 2009

W ITH Duke still on board we roll into *La Paz*, eager to hop the ferry to mainland Mexico. After confirming at an office in town, it's another thirty minutes along the beautiful coastline to the ferry terminal at *Pichilingue* where I get busy waiting in a long line of people trying to complete Customs paperwork. At the front of the line a lady is transporting eight vehicles at once, so I wait impatiently for over an hour. When my turn comes the girl behind the counter asks in English if I speak Spanish, and I reply no. I ask in Spanish if she speaks English, and she replies no. After a little nervous laughter on both sides we simply don't let the language barrier get in the way.

Mexico loves bureaucracy, and I need multiple copies of all my various forms and documents. I have everything required except the Tourist Card issued half way down Baja. Luckily, I am allowed back to the front of the line after dashing to a photocopier around the corner. I sign a few forms, pay $30 USD and in less than ten minutes I am issued a shiny sticker for the windshield of the Jeep, officially allowing me to drive throughout Mexico for the duration of my Tourist Card.

Now the Jeep is legally permitted onto the mainland, we tackle the next hurdle - ferry tickets. It seems the ferry companies go bankrupt and change hands every year or two, so my planning is way off the mark in terms of schedules and prices. Our options are the more expensive Baja Ferries, or the cheaper Transportation Maritime of California. By some fluke of luck the latter has a ferry leaving in a few hours. After some back and forward to determine if we will fit, we are given the all-clear. A ticket for myself and the Jeep costs $227 USD, while Duke pays $62 USD for a walk-on passenger ticket.

I drive through huge formidable-looking gates where a Customs inspector has a good look at the Jeep's new sticker, verifies the VIN number and then asks if I am me, which I think is obvious.

Rounding a building we see our home for the next sixteen hours, a huge old vehicle ferry named *La San Guillermo*. Judging by the rust and grime, she has clearly entered old-age. The loading guys immediately wave me aboard, onto a hydraulic lift built into the vessel. The lift brings the Jeep to the upper deck, already half full of tightly packed 18-wheelers and transport trucks. The Jeep is the smallest vehicle by a long margin and is quickly sandwiched between the heavily loaded trucks. I am happy to see each truck is secured to the open deck with heavy chains - even a slight movement in any direction would spell disaster for the little Jeep.

Purchasing the cheapest possible tickets means we don't have our own cabin, so we must roam the ship to find whatever space is available. One large room is provided for cattle class passengers, and is filling fast by the time we find it. The truck drivers are obviously well practiced in this routine and have stripped the seats of cushions and are already sound asleep, sprawled around the floor. The air in the room is already stale, and snoring seems to be a local contest, making me quickly decide this is not the place for us.

For entertainment before departure we all watch the loading process continue from the back deck. Each new truck is pushed within inches on all sides, and it's clear those gathered are waiting for a mishap. When all agree the upper deck is full, yet another 18-wheeler is brought up. I don't need to speak Spanish to understand I'm not the only one who thinks it won't fit.

The driver reverses off the lift until the rear of the trailer is exactly where he wants it, leaving the front sticking out sideways about twelve feet. The prime mover is then disconnected from the trailer, before making a fifteen-point turn. It is then reconnected to the trailer at a right angle, something I have never seen before. The driver is obviously in a very low gear as he revs the engine hard and reverses, slowly forcing the fully loaded trailer to slide sideways into the small space. All of us spectators stand to get a better view of the screeching tires and howling engine. Many nods of approval are seen as the trailer comes to a stop in a gap that can not be more than three inches longer than the trailer itself.
A neat trick, for sure.

We sit on the open deck to watch the crew cast off before powering out into the calm, open ocean. Striking up a conversation with guys our age soon draws a small crowd of drivers. We use my pocket dictionary to conjure up all sorts of horribly broken sentences in Spanish, which nobody seems to care about. The drivers find us immensely entertaining, and the feeling is mutual. They quickly befriend us, and soon extend a dinner invite. We are elated to learn a meal in the galley is included in the ticket price. Dinner is a heaping plate of rice, chicken and re-fried beans wrapped in corn tortillas. Needless to say everything is spicy beyond belief, which hits the spot perfectly. Duke and I share soda, cookies and beer with the drivers until we are kicked out of the galley at closing time.

Not wanting to say goodnight just yet, we find a quiet spot out of the wind where we continue chatting to the drivers late into the night. I'm curious about the life of a Mexican trucker, and how each of them makes the ferry trip from Baja to Mainland Mexico at least twice a week. It's a slow process on both sides to continually look up words in the dictionary, though being stuck on a ferry with nothing else to do means we have patience to spare. The drivers can't believe I live out of my tiny Jeep, and they wonder why I am not living in the United States, given I can legally go there. From what I can tell, many Mexicans view the United States as paradise, and would jump at the chance to live there. It sounds like even just visiting the US is difficult for these men.

Eventually I explain my plan to drive to South America, causing even more confusion. They find it difficult to believe I could save enough money in just two years and therefore assume I must be rich. Even after I explain I cook all my own food and sleep in a tent on the ground, I can't convince them otherwise. It's hard to accept them thinking I am rich, though I figure it's something I will have to get used to. We bid goodnight to our new friends after many more hours of noisy chatter.

The night air is perfectly warm so I find a quiet place on deck to roll out my sleeping mat. As soon as I lie down I feel the slight rocking of the ship across the ocean for the first time. This gentle movement is most noticeable as I search for familiar star constellations in the staggering number visible. I lie awake thinking about the enormity of where I am and what I am doing.

My head has been buzzing all afternoon at the situation I find myself in. I'm riding the biggest ferry of my life. I'm in a foreign country where I don't speak the language. I'm meeting friendly people everywhere I go and I'm enjoying myself immensely. For the first time the scale of what I am doing fully sinks in. I also realize this journey is only growing larger every day.

Driving North to the Arctic Ocean and exploring the West Coast of Canada and the USA was an amazing adventure in itself. During that time I always felt the adventure was well within my abilities and everything was familiar, in a sense. After months on the road I fell into routines, and each day I mostly knew what to expect. Now, on this ferry in Mexico, I sense something has changed. Somehow the adventure has moved up into a whole new category - a category I have never before ventured into. I am pushing beyond my comfort zone, and I feel certain both the difficulties and rewards will be much higher.

I start to understand how Ted Simon must have felt, pushing into the unknown. The knowledge that his journey was successful is comforting, and I again feel inspired by his courage and determination.

Ψ   Ψ   Ψ

I wake with the first light of dawn, and lie in my sleeping bag for half an hour watching a pod of dolphins play beside the ship. Birds squabble noisily as they jostle for position on the hand rails, and I spot a couple of huge turtles floating by. We enjoy a delicious and spicy breakfast of beans and rice with our new trucker friends, picking up the conversation where we left off last night. When *La San Guillermo* rumbles into *Mazatlan* soon after sunrise, we wish each other all the best for the road ahead.

The entire loading process is run in reverse, and soon we find ourselves wide eyed on the streets of *Mazatlan* on a beautiful sunny day. Without any kind of map, we are soon hopelessly lost in the maze of narrow streets.

Mainland Mexico and Central America, here I come!

An Introduction To Corruption

Puerto Vallarta, Central Mexico
November 2009

D UKE and I have had a great run in Mexico. On the Baja we were on the beach every day, and on the mainland we have been hopping around, meeting other travellers and having the time of our lives. The sun is warm, the beer is cold and cheap, and we have become addicted to five cent street tacos that are shockingly spicy. So far, the Police have completely ignored us. Neither of us thought for a second that would continue.

Everyone says the main drag of *Puerto Vallarta* is fantastic at night, and we are eager to look around. After a few beers we set off on a little adventure with Ben and Mike, a couple of Aussie backpackers. José, a local we met a couple of hours ago also tags along. He lives in the area, and apparently comes to the hostel to mingle with backpackers and have a laugh.

The guys light up a joint and smoke as we walk, which José assures us is not a problem in Mexico. We are also drinking beer while laughing together and generally enjoying the warm evening. José leads the way through a labyrinth of narrow, winding residential streets, and quickly we become dependant on him for directions. Suddenly, a Police pickup tears around a corner, blocking our path as it screeches to a halt.

Two uniformed Police quickly grab our hands to smell them, asking if we have been smoking anything tonight. It becomes very obvious they can tell who has been smoking and who has not. Quickly and efficiently, they line everyone up to be frisked, hands on the hood of the pickup.

The frisking starts at the far end of the line up, so I have time to size up the situation. The two Policeman are dressed in immaculate uniforms, and each sport a bushy mustache above wide grins. They both display medals and ribbons on their shoulders and chests, something they are clearly proud of. In stark contrast their pickup is old and battered, virtually falling apart.

I have never been detained by Police like this in my life, though I don't feel scared or threatened at all. I'm not sure if it's the beer or the relaxed atmosphere, but I actually find it all quite amusing. I'm so relaxed, in fact, I continue to drink my beer, using the hood of the pickup as a table. I have not been smoking, so the Policemen are not at all interested in me. The only hint this is serious comes when I walk behind one of the officers, who puts his hand protectively on his sidearm and gives me a meaningful look. The tone is relaxed, though he clearly doesn't want to risk me snatching his weapon.

When my turn comes, the officer meticiously frisks me. After digging it out of my pocket, he goes to work on my almost-empty wallet. I intentionally have only $10 USD worth of Pesos, a copy of my drivers license and a few old business cards. This is my strategy to mitigate the consequences of theft - I don't care if it gets stolen. I also don't have the keys to the Jeep with me, so they can't be stolen either. The officer opens every compartment, emptying the meager contents on the hood of the pickup. I find it curious when he makes me take out my cash and hold onto it while continuing his search. I'm later told if he blatantly takes money from me I can launch a formal complaint and there are serious consequences for stealing from a tourist so obviously. He makes a big show of having me hold onto my money, not wanting to risk any confusion about stealing from me.

Ten minutes later, after everyone has been frisked, the thorough search turns up nothing. Clearly frustrated, the Police demand money.
For what, we don't really know.

Suddenly, just as quickly as they came, they jump into the pickup and disappear in a cloud of exhaust smoke, leaving us to wonder what exactly just happened.

A few hundred yards later we hear tires squeal and the same Police zoom around the nearest corner to demand money once again. We are later told they don't want locals to see them creating a scene and extorting money from tourists. Trying to be inconspicuous, they keep moving to different places before repeating their demands. This charade is repeated twice more before it's crystal clear they will not leave us alone until we pay them off.
Exactly how much they want is difficult to say.

With his perfect Spanish and apparent clear understanding of the situation, José takes the lead on negotiating, translating and explaining what's going on. José says if we don't pay, the Police will throw us in a local jail for the night to think about it. José assures us this will be extremely unpleasant for white guys like us. After still more back and forward the two smokers eventually hand over 100 pesos each (about $8 USD), which turns into another big charade. The officer angrily snatches the money and throws it on the floor of the pickup looking disgusted. He then launches into a speech about how he is actually the good guy here. If he wasn't 'helping' us, we would all be in Federal Prison for the night and would wind up paying ten times more money to get out. He makes it crystal clear just how nasty Federal Prison would be. In fact, he explains, we're all fortunate he came along to help and we should be thanking him for being such a nice guy.

Yeah, right.

The Police screech away into the night as quickly as they came, leaving us to again wonder when they will return. Talking around what just happened as we continue into town, we realize it only cost our group $16 USD for our first lesson in Police corruption. All things considered, that's a cheap and easy lesson.

I can't help thinking how José was cool, calm and collected during the whole encounter. While taking on translator duties, he was also extremely quick to side with the Police. I'm pretty sure he sold the joint to Ben and Mike and I think it might even have been José who finally convinced us to pay.

Was José also on the take?
To this day I have absolutely no idea.

Border Crossings

Central America
Early 2010

P EOPLE often ask about the border crossings in Central
America.
How intense are they?
How many times did I pay bribes?
Did I have guns pointed at me?
Even now I meet people who insist some of the borders are
impossible to cross with a vehicle - the very borders I crossed.
All I can do is respectfully disagree.

Following is a collection of the most memorable border crossings from Central America. Some are stories from the beginning of the journey when I was green and didn't know how to
play the game. Others are stories which taught me valuable
lessons that serve me to this day.

Into Belize

I have been exploring Mexico for almost two months, loving every minute. The landscapes, sights and people have been nothing short of brilliant. I could eat spicy street tacos every day for the rest of my life and be a very happy person. Despite how much I have enjoyed Mexico, I need to keep moving.

I leave Duke at the airport in *Guadalajara*, and a month later I pick up my friend Kate at the *Cancún* airport. Kate and I went to University together, and although we have not seen each other for a few years, we know our friendship will survive six weeks on the road through Southern Mexico, Belize and Guatemala.

Not ready to leave just yet, we make one last stop in Mexico for lunch in the town of *Chetumal*. We find a beautiful spot directly on the ocean, complete with green grass and picnic tables. The warm sun, seagulls and cleanliness have me feeling nostalgic for Australia. I could be in any of the picturesque beach towns Downunder.

The entertainment comes when Kate tries a concrete slide that ends abruptly in the shallow ocean. The shiny concrete is slick, giving Kate no chance to slow down, much less stop. The three foot drop at the end is actually her downfall. In a valiant attempt, Kate begins running in mid air as she shoots off the end of the slide. Unfortunately her legs are simply not moving fast enough, causing her to face plant into about a foot of water with a sandy bottom. I am relieved when she comes up laughing, and we both don't stop for a long while.

Moving South we arrive at the border much sooner than I expect, making me feel rushed and unprepared. I have heard endless horror stories of hours of paperwork, bribery and lawlessness at Central American borders. In an attempt to avoid these problems, I planned to prepare myself and my paperwork as much as possible before arriving at each border. It's too late for that now.

Soon we are stuck in a line of cars and trucks, all jostling to move through huge steel gates I assume are the exit of Mexico. All the idling vehicles belch black smoke, fortifying the thick, sticky air. The temperature is well over a hundred in the shade, and my clothes cling to me in the intense humidity. Hundreds of people mill about, weaving in and out of traffic selling cold drinks and deep-fried snacks through open windows. Yet more people are trudging through the gates, carrying food, water, children, clothes and even live animals on their backs. Military men in full riot gear stand on the edges, scanning back and forward across the crowd. Each man looks stern and serious while holding an assault rifle at the ready.

I have never before witnessed a scene like this, and I feel an odd combination of anxiety, apprehension and excitement.

An official looking man wearing an immaculate shirt and tie directs me to pull to the side. He says I must purchase car insurance before entering Belize, saying it is mandatory by law. I get a bit flustered, not certain what is going on or what I should do. I know insurance is required in Belize, and this guy looks legit, so I hand over my Registration and Drivers Licence before he walks out of sight.

Immediately I know I have made a mistake - I should have asked more questions before handing over my paperwork.
Who is this guy?
Why am I getting Belize Insurance before I have left Mexico?
Something feels wrong.

I feel a little better with the knowledge the two documents I gave him are both color photocopies - the originals are safely locked in the Jeep. Even still, for the next ten minutes my mind runs through the sinister things he might be doing with my paperwork. Maybe he is transferring ownership of the Jeep. Maybe he is posing as me for some reason. Maybe I will never see him, or my paperwork again. I feel like I'm drowning as I race through two hundred other far-fetched ideas that put me on edge.

While waiting, we line up for an exit stamp in our passports from Mexican Immigration. The line ends at a ramshackle hut with a tiny window where I can barely see a lone man hunched over a battered table, apparently an official. He wears a grubby uniform that I can smell through the window. Kate pays one hundred Pesos for the stamp (less than $10 USD). Watching carefully, I see a gleam in his eyes as he throws Kate's money onto a huge pile of grubby bills on the table. He then says I must pay two hundred and sixty-two Pesos for the same stamp (around $20 USD). When I hand over five hundred Pesos, he throws it on the same pile and gives me two hundred and fifty Pesos change, not the correct change for the price he said.

We have no idea why we had to pay this money and receive no receipt. Further, I have no idea why I paid more than Kate for the same stamp.

I sit on the Jeep to wait for the man with my documents to return, still feeling anxious. With time to think, I carefully watch everything around me. I notice locals are not paying for the exit stamp. In fact, they are not even talking to the man in the hut. Others are getting the stamp without paying a cent.

I think we just got scammed.
Scratch that, I am certain we just got scammed.
Lesson learned.

Eventually, the man in the shirt and tie returns with paperwork he wants me to sign - apparently Belize vehicle insurance. Now wary from my exit stamp experience, I have my head on straight and spend a long time reading his paperwork. The document is written in English, and looks legit. The man insets I sign as quickly as possible and his urgency makes me feel something is not right. When I ask about the price, he throws out a huge number in Pesos. This is strange, because the price is clearly written on the policy in Belize Dollars, which kicks off a long argument about the exchange rate.

I'm certain the Belize Dollar is pegged 2:1 to the US Dollar, so I know it's value. His steadfast insistence has me questioning myself, however, and I wish I had prepared better.

His credibility falls apart when he suddenly cuts his asking price in half. Even still, it's higher than the price written on the policy. When I react badly to that, he asks
"How much do you want to pay?"

I was already suspicious of this man, and this is the last straw. This has gone too far. I tell him I'm not interested, and try to walk away. At this he becomes agitated, grabbing my arm and insisting I must sign immediately.
I will not sign.

I feel extremely uncomfortable that he has official-looking paperwork with my name, license number and the VIN of my Jeep. I am also getting angry as the yelling escalates on both sides.

Finally, I put an end to the nonsense by tearing the policy into shreds right in front of him. He completely flips out and screams that he is going to have the Military arrest me, before storming away with the shredded paperwork stuffed in his pockets.

I have my documents back, so I ignore him and drive on.

After the massive gates signifying the exit of Mexico, we enter the no-mans-land between the two countries. We have been stamped out of Mexico, but have not yet entered Belize. Officially, we are in no country. I doubt the law of either would get involved here. There are again thousands of people milling about buying and selling food, clothes, live animals and crate after crate of tinned goods. Hundreds of men eye the Jeep as we slowly roll by.
I don't like this place one bit.

I think it's best to resolve my insurance woes, so I stop at a shack, apparently the office of the insurance company whose papers I shredded. As I step from the Jeep, the man runs up, still yelling and waiving his arms furiously. Inside, the lady at the desk is very friendly as I try my best to be polite and speak calmly and slowly, making a conscious effort to calm myself. This proves to be extremely difficult when the man also comes inside, ranting and raving loudly. He will not let me get a word in sideways. Finally, after both the lady and I have told him to be quiet ten times each, he sits quietly while I tell the story.

It soon becomes clear this lady is selling legitimate insurance, and the man is a kind of opportunistic broker. He ran across and bought a policy in my name for two hundred Pesos, before running back to charge me five hundred Pesos. The nice lady is utterly shocked when I tell her I shredded the policy. Flustered, she eventually calls her supervisor to sort it out.

In the end, everything works out. The kind lady takes the shredded paperwork and gives the man back his two hundred Pesos and we can all pretend the whole thing never happened. Hilariously, she has been instructed not to sell me another policy.

Two hurdles down, we move forward to a 'fumigation' stop for the Jeep - this is likely another scam - this time one I have been warned about. Some chemical is sprayed on the outside of the Jeep, apparently to stop the spread of some animal disease or other. It could easily be just water for all I know. The whole thing is semi-official and I do get a receipt for my eighty pesos ($6 USD), so I pay without argument. I park at the edge of no-mans-land and walk inside to Belize Immigration. Here we both get entry stamps without issue and I move onto Customs to complete paperwork for the Jeep. They put a huge stamp in my passport which prevents me leaving Belize without the Jeep - an attempt to stop people selling vehicles illegally. When we finally drive into Belize I decide it is best to buy insurance, this time from a large office that charges the correct price.

Right at sunset we're free to drive into Belize, excited to explore a new country.

Into Guatemala

After a fantastic couple of weeks in Belize, Kate and I move West to the major border just outside *San Ignacio*. In town we bump into Rupert and Amy, an Australian couple driving an '89 Range Rover around the world. They have just come North through every country in Central and South America and so we have tons of information to share on both sides. It's invigorating to meet people that have just done what I am attempting - proving it really is possible and I'm probably not as crazy as some people think. My mind works overtime for the rest of the day, full of adventures to come.

The border itself is on the banks of a small river, with a large building on either side serving double duty as Immigration and Customs. A few people and vehicles are moving in each direction, though it is nothing like the chaotic scene when we entered Belize. First we must pay a $37.50 BZ ($19 USD) departure tax just for permission to leave Belize. I am given a fancy receipt and I remember reading online this is legit. At Customs the special stamp in my passport is canceled without a problem.

Now free to leave, we drive a hundred yards to begin the process of entering Guatemala.

I once again pay for fumigation of the Jeep, and make sure to get a receipt for my $3 USD. We stand in line at Immigration with a handful of other people, waiting for an entrance stamp. My research says we can get a CA-4 stamp that allows free travel between Guatemala, El Salvador, Honduras and Nicaragua for a total of 90 days, and it should be free.

After stamping our passports, the border official behind a large desk asks for 20 Quetzales (about $2.50 USD) for each stamp. Now hyper-alert to this scam, I am certain this is not official.

I smile and politely ask for a receipt, which amazingly he can not give. Over the course of five minutes he goes through every excuse in the book - we don't issue receipts here, the computer does not work, the printer does not work, the printer is out of ink, the printer is out of paper. After each excuse I politely smile and again ask for a receipt. I explain it is simply impossible for me to pay an official fee to an official without an official receipt.

This standoff continues while the line behind me grows longer and longer. I intentionally block access to those behind me so they can't reach around with their documents. I continue to smile and wait patiently, all the while asking politely for a receipt. Eventually the border official hands our two passports to his supervisor who again says we must pay. Again I explain I can not pay an official without an official receipt, causing him to scowl sternly. Clearly unhappy, he throws the two passports directly at me. I make no attempt to catch them, so they bounce off my chest and land in the dirt. The two officers turn and walk away without a backwards glance, leaving me to collect them.

I'm learning.

Into El Salvador

After almost a month exploring Guatemala together, Kate and I venture into Guatemala City so Kate can catch a plane home. We find a great place to stay near the airport for her last night, though I can't help noticing all the buildings have electrified razor wire on top of twelve foot concrete fences. The electricity certainly adds a nice little something. Kate leaves early in the morning and it's a strange feeling to be on my own again. Both exciting and a little lonely.

I move Southeast to a small border near the village of *Valle Nuevo*. I have intentionally turned off the main road because I want to explore smaller roads and places less visited. From

a distance, the border appears to be a laid-back, sleepy affair, with almost no traffic and less than a hundred people milling around.
I'm still a hundred yards from the main building when ten men run and completely surround the Jeep.

Straight away I have my guard up, and feel intimidated to have the men physically blocking my way forward or back. My window is down and immediately hands reach inside, grabbing for my paperwork. I scramble to lock doors and wind windows up, before they can actually get hold of anything. Through a crack in the window the men demand my passport and vehicle paperwork, which further raises my suspicions. None of the men are wearing uniforms, though a couple show me 'ID badges' hanging around their necks. When I look closely I see they are obviously homemade, worse than my color photocopies.

I have no intention of handing over any documents to this rag-tag bunch, though I do need to exchange money and they appear to be the only option. After a lot of negotiation I carefully count each bill twice before I'm satisfied, and the exchange is made without a problem. Time and again I say I don't want their help to cross the border, though they will not leave me alone. A few stick to me like glue, following on foot as I drive further forward and park directly in front of the main building where I will be able to see the Jeep.

I ask the first uniformed officer for guidance about how to proceed. One of my followers pesters us by continually butting into the conversation - he simply will not let me get a word in or leave me alone. Losing patience, I finally tell him to shut up before I turn back to the armed guard and politely ask him to continue. The guard smiles and nods before explaining exactly where I need to go.

While waiting in line for an exit stamp, I have a minute of quiet to think, and I remember stories about these men that won't stop pestering me. Under the guise of 'assisting' to cross the border they do whatever it takes to get a person's paperwork. They tell all kinds of tall tales about how difficult and expensive the border crossing will be without their assistance and translations. Taking them on their word, many foreigners gladly accept their 'help', thinking it will ease the process. Once in control of the paperwork, they often invent fees and repeatedly ask for more money to pass each step. They are often in cahoots with everyone at the border and get a cut of each 'fee' paid. When finally clear of the border, they ask for their fee, and will not return documents until it is paid. Stories abound of demands for $100 USD or more. With no choice, foreigners often wind up paying to get their documents back. These guys are commonly called 'Fixers' or 'Border Helpers' and while they are not all rip-off merchants, I've heard enough stories to stay well clear.

My thinking is confirmed when they finally realize I'm not going to take the bait. I watch with amusement as the men swarm towards the next vehicles arriving and attempt to hook a prize.

In less than twenty minutes I finish the formalities to leave Guatemala and cross a deep valley into El Salvador. At Immigration the officer briefly glances at my CA-4 stamp before waiving me away, and Customs type up the Jeep details and issue me a three month permit. Everything is easy and free.

Driving away into El Salvador, I reflect on the border crossing. I'm pleased I kept my head on my shoulders, and easily completed the required steps without a Fixer and without paying a cent.

I decide my new goal is to cross every border without paying for a single fixer, and I feel certain patience is the key.

Into Costa Rica

I have been warned repeatedly about the border crossing from Nicaragua into Costa Rica. This border especially is rumored to be a nightmare of bureaucracy, and is convoluted enough to break even seasoned Overlanders. There are stories of sleeping multiple nights in the border area attempting to complete the required steps just to leave Nicaragua. Countless people have told me this is the worst border in Central America. With all of this in mind, I prepare for a long haul as I approach the border at *Peñas Blancas.*

I drive past a line of trucks stretching well over a mile, apparently all trying to cross which surely can't be a good sign. At the front of the line a uniformed officer waves me down, and I pay $1 USD for some kind of official stamp. When I try to get into the Jeep, the officer stops me and points to a nearby shack. There another uniformed man hands me a tiny scrap of grubby paper with the license plate of the Jeep and today's date scrawled in barely legible writing. When I ask the guard "Where next?", he points silently before turning to deal with the next vehicle.

I'm directed to drive behind a huge building where the real chaos begins in a massive parking lot. There are hundreds of cars, buses and trucks crammed into every available square inch. In the gaps between vehicles thousands of people mill about, apparently not going anywhere in particular. All carry huge sacks of the usual fare - food, water, clothes, children, and live animals stuffed into impossibly small cages.

The second I step from the Jeep, multiple men rush forward and yell directly in my face while trying to snatch my paperwork. Clearly they are fixers, though these men are much more aggressive than any I have seen before. Now with a few more crossings under my belt, I have learned the best way of dealing with these guys. I repeatedly say I don't want help and pretend not to be interested. I also work hard on keeping a smile on my face, speaking calmly and politely and acting confident. I then listen carefully while they inevitably shout the next step I must complete, apparently trying to show how smart they are. If I get stuck and spend even five seconds pondering the next step, another fixer leaps forward to yell the next step.

Again, I say no thanks before moving along.

By chance I bump into a Customs officer wandering the crowd and hand him my scrap of paper, hoping he will know what to do. He glances briefly at the Jeep before scribbling his name on the scrap. Next I find a Policeman who does exactly the same thing, though he doesn't even look at the Jeep. Clutching my precious scrap of paper, I move inside a large crowded building. Here I find my way into a long line of people who are apparently trying to achieve a similar goal. I strike up a conversation with a local who assures me this is the correct place for me. Together with others in line, it is agreed I have so far jumped through the correct hoops in the correct order.

After about twenty minutes it becomes clear that waiting in line is not an important concept here. Many people push in and out of lines every which way and reach over to skip ahead. My new friend sees an opening and together we rush to the front of a newly-opened window, quickly shoving our paperwork through before anyone else can. Here, my permit for the Jeep is thrown on a pile and I get a new scribble and even a stamp on my scrap of paper. To explain the next step, the extremely bored-looking lady merely points to the next line across. Forty minutes later when I reach the front of that line, the same process is repeated, netting me yet another illegible scribble and stamp on my now filthy scrap of paper.

I'm not at all certain, though I think the process for the Jeep might be complete, meaning it can legally leave Nicaragua. Probably. Now I just have to figure out how to get myself stamped out.

With the worst possible timing, a couple of packed buses pull in, instantly turning Immigration into a zoo. After waiting and watching for forty-five minutes, I have no trouble completing a tourist card and paying $2 USD for an exit stamp allowing me to also leave.

Eager to see if I have completed everything correctly, I jump in

the Jeep and wade through the sea of people. The final guard manning the boom gate barely glances at my grubby scrap of paper before waiving me through. I watch as he tosses it on an enormous pile of similar-looking scraps.
Bureaucracy at it's finest!

After all of that, I have left Nicaragua and pass through a small no-mans-land. Now I must enter Costa Rica.

Fumigation is first and I'm surprised when the guy waves me right in without paying. I only hope I won't need a receipt for that later. I park at the main Immigration building where I wait in another huge line of bus passengers to get myself into the country. Another forty-five minutes and another tourist card later I'm rewarded with an entrance stamp.

In the adjacent room I pay $15 USD for mandatory car insurance and get a photocopy of my new passport stamp. Customs are happy to take the copy and insurance policy and issue me a hand written permit for the Jeep. A Policeman has a brief look inside before indicating where I must go next.

A short drive away I stand in yet another line at a nondescript white building, hopefully the final hurdle. All the paperwork I have accumulated so far is typed and given back to me as a formal-looking document permitting the Jeep in Costa Rica.

The crossing has taken many hours in sweltering heat, though it could have been much worse. This border has been repeatedly hyped as the worst I will encounter in all of The Americas, yet the reality turned out to be quite different.

Ψ   Ψ   Ψ

None of the borders are seriously horrible, and certainly none are remotely close to impossible. There is absolutely no need to pay for fixers.

With the right attitude - a friendly smile and a good deal of patience - nothing is a problem.

The weekend before I quit my job in Calgary

The Magic Bus, near Mount McKinley, Alaska

Paddling with the icebergs of Colombia Glacier, Alaska

Mike and Dan starting The West Coast Trail, Vancouver Island

Using a Spanish dictionary to chat with a Mexican trucker

A typical Mexican beach town. Paradise!

Exploring remote beaches on Mexico's mainland

The warning sign on Pacaya Volcano

Welcome to Honduras

Playing With Lava

Volcán Pacaya, Guatemala
February 2010

T HE temptation to get extremely close to flowing lava is
much too strong to pass up. In fact it's something I never
imagined I would do in my life. I thought lava was reserved for
National Geographic sponsored expeditions at astronomical
cost. As it turns out, I was completely wrong.

Hiking *Volcán Pacaya* is a simple day trip from *Antigua*, and
I decide to pay $12 USD for a group tour. The tour means
I can forget about navigation and driving for the afternoon -
sometimes it's nice to leave the Jeep behind and relax while
looking around. On the advice of many, I choose the afternoon
tour, with the hope of seeing the glowing lava at sunset.

After booking the tour, I stop to browse in a small bookshop.
I'm completely disoriented when the bookshelves start rocking
away from the walls towards the center of the room, and then

back to the walls. It takes me a second to realize what's happening - an earthquake. I dart outside, just in time to see power poles swaying back and forth, causing the wires to go slack then tight. It's surreal to think strong winds can not make this happen, but it's happening now. The ground also moves slightly, somewhat similar to being on a large boat in the ocean. A fellow observer tries desperately to curb my obvious enthusiasm - it's probably not tactful to say earthquakes are cool while in a city that has been completely destroyed more than once.

Ψ   Ψ   Ψ

Only ninety minutes after leaving *Antigua* - the last thirty seriously uphill - we pile out of the minibus, ready to hike. Instantly we are swarmed by children selling all sorts of stuff we don't need. They relentlessly chant "is necessary" until eventually a couple of people give in and buy walking sticks. The children are also selling bottled water, which makes sense, though I don't understand why they're hawking bags of marsh-mallows. After all, we're going hiking here.

Soon enough we begin trudging up the steep and dusty trail in the scorching afternoon sun. Hiking is my favourite activity of all time, so I'm truly in my element and enjoy every minute. I continually rush to the front to talk to people, before slowing down to chat to others further back. My well-worn leather hiking boots are as comfortable as warm socks, and I'm soon munching and sharing my snacks of trail mix, chocolate and granola bars.

My Spanish has been ever-so-slowly improving since Mexico, and I'm now confident enough to blurt out sentences and watch the reaction. I'm extremely proud when I more-or-less understand what our guide says about the volcano - how often it erupts and how dangerous it is. I'm also able to mostly read the sign in Spanish explaining all of this, which again feels like a huge accomplishment.

Over a couple of hours the hike slowly changes from dry and dusty sand to small volcanic pebbles, then huge volcanic boulders with razor sharp pieces jutting out. We climb above cloud level and are treated to spectacular views of *Volcán Fuego* (Fire). This nearby volcano is visible from downtown *Antigua* spewing clouds of black smoke and ash every hour or two.

The scramble quickly becomes congested as about sixty tourists try to climb together. I'm uncomfortable with so many hikers on the extremely unstable rocks that are constantly being kicked, causing them to rain down on those below. I know we are getting close to the action when the rocks under my feet get hotter and hotter. Eventually I can't use my hands for balance anymore - the rocks are too hot to touch - and I sweat profusely. Occasionally a strong sulphur smell wafts past, adding to the general excitement, and certain knowledge we are approaching something amazing.

I stop for a breather and have a good look at what lies ahead. Messing with my vision, huge waves of heat haze roll off the mountain around me, forcing me to take in the seriousness of my surroundings. Adding to my uneasiness, our guide says the odd-colored rocks I'm standing on were flowing lava only last week!

I reach a point where about fifty people are milling around and I'm taken completely by surprise to see a river of red hot lava less than fifteen feet away. I climb to a high point, putting me about ten feet away from the small flow. The lava looks like bright red sludge, slowly sliding down the mountainside. I can see it's quite thick, flowing slowly like cold honey.

My brain can hardly process what is in front of me and it takes thirty seconds to fully comprehend what I'm looking at. Heat pours off the lava in thick waves, causing me to sweat more and more. When the wind changes my exposed legs and face sting, forcing me to scramble back as quickly as I can. Doing so makes me aware of the forty people still climbing, and how over-crowded the area is already.

Needing to do something about my exposed skin, I move down and away to a lower vantage point where I put on long pants and guzzle water. This turns out to be an amazingly good idea when more and more people pack onto the extremely hot and uneven rocky surface. More than once when the wind changes people slip and panic trying to scramble away from the heat waves. With more people crowding in behind they have nowhere to go. Soon panic erupts as people try to scramble away on the slippery razor-sharp rocks. Many anxious faces can be seen when thin-soled shoes begin to melt and stick to the rocks. The fumes of the melting plastic and rubber combine with the strong odor of sulfur creating an overpowering - and probably toxic - stench.

I stand on my little platform chatting to various people and roasting marshmallows. Yep, now I know why kids were selling them at the bottom of the mountain. It's pure genius to roast marshmallows on lava. From where I stand I can poke a marshmallow on a stick through cracks in the rock towards the lava beneath my feet. In just a few seconds it is roasted to perfection, and I don't even need to move to enjoy the magic. Roasting them on coals is fine and all, but it can't touch the taste of the lava roasted variety. This might just ruin regular old flame-roasted for me.

A few people have moved about thirty yards further, and after getting a report I know I have to check it out. To hike up I carefully hop from rock to rock with red hot lava visible in the gaps between each. I am strongly reminded of countless video games where the player must hop over lava to avoid certain death. While the lava between the rocks is not bubbling like in the games, there is still absolutely zero room for error here.

I reach a rocky area where the temperature is bearable, less than six feet from a much larger flow of lava. I stand and stare in awe at the liquid rock - truly breathtaking and hard to comprehend. A river at least ten feet wide is sliding down the mountain, moving at a slow walk. The lava is a dark red, and often the surface is close to black. Tumbling slightly, the lava seems to roll as much as it slides. Looking carefully I can see the parts exposed to the air are darker, while the inside is a much brighter red that is visible when the outer layer tumbles and slides off.

When the wind changes I'm forced to turn my back in an attempt to protect my face and hands. Both feel badly sunburned purely from the intense air temperature. I'm especially curious about the consistency of the lava, so I throw rocks into the river to see what happens. I am surprised to see the rocks either bounce off, or sit on top - apparently the lava has a hard invisible shell. After sitting for about ten seconds the rocks slowly melt down into the lava, turning it a murky dark brown.

Marshmallows and sticks burst into flame and are vaporized instantly upon direct contact. The tip of the roasting stick simply vanishes as quickly as I feed it in. I am completely captivated and wish I had more things to shove into the lava.

The sun dips below the horizon, giving way to a spectacular sunset. Visible lava increases ten fold in the fading light and everyone reluctantly starts moving downhill - everyone except me. I want to draw out the experience, confident I can scramble down quickly.

I stay as long as possible, taking long exposure photos. I can now see lava completely surrounds me, and is also clearly visible on the nearby mountains. In the quickly fading light the whole area comes to life, blazing red all around. There is a hundred times more liquid lava than I thought. I could happily stay here all night watching it slowly inch down the mountain. After all, being cold is not a problem. Unfortunately, my group is now far ahead, so I hike double time to catch up, basically running down the mountain.

To this day hiking *Volcán Pacaya* to play with lava remains one of the top ten natural experiences of my life. Being in such close contact with naturally liquid rock gave me an overwhelming sense of just how alive the earth actually is. I'm also acutely aware it has been this way for billions of years, and will continue long after I am gone.

Even now it's difficult to roast marshmallows on a campfire without longing for the far superior lava-roasted variety.

On Missing Out

LIVING a fulfilling and enjoyable life is something we all strive for, each and every day. Obviously, we all have different definitions of that, with no definition being more correct, or better, than any other. Each of us take our own path, make our own decisions, and discover our own definitions of fulfilment and enjoyment. During my journey, time and time again my own definitions were challenged, forcing me to re-evaluate what I wanted from life.

Central America is absolutely bursting with things to do and magical places to see every single day. Stunning beaches, waterfalls, sand boarding, ancient temples, mountains, snorkeling and scuba diving. I could go on all day - the list really is endless. Given unlimited time and money, it might *just* be possible to see everything, but even that I can not guarantee. With each activity completed, the list of future activities is always longer, never shorter.

Over time, the realization there are things I will not see and experience on this trip slowly eats away at me. There are days when I feel almost desperate about visiting some place or doing an activity - no matter what. Even in the pouring rain I'm determined to visit waterfalls, and hiking to the top of mountains in thick fog becomes a strange habit.

I'm aware I have always struggled with a Fear Of Missing Out (FOMO). Central America and the endless activities on offer has apparently amplified my FOMO, which had always been lurking just below the surface.

In fact, FOMO is a major reason I set out on this journey to begin with. When I really think about it, I'm fully aware this is my attempt to 'do and see everything', as crazy as that sounds.

My journey from Alaska to Argentina has two major constraints. Time in each country is limited by visas, and I am acutely aware my savings will run out sooner or later. These constraints means it's an impossibility for me to see and do everything, and I have to come to terms with that.

Somehow, I still want to cram everything into an ever decreasing amount of time.

$$\Psi \quad \Psi \quad \Psi$$

One particularly jarring case of FOMO comes in the evening immediately after playing with lava on *Volcán Pacaya*. Still high on adrenaline after one of the best experiences of my life, I head out for a drink. Inevitably I meet other Western travellers bursting with stories of adventure. Quickly we are swapping stories, and one particularly loud guy declares we have all severely 'missed out' today. He went sand boarding, and it was amazing. Actually, it was more than amazing, it was life-changing. So life-changing was his day, that he spends the next twenty minutes loudly telling everyone about it.

By the end of his rant I actually feel as if I missed out. Somehow, he has me convinced that sand boarding really is the best thing on earth and everyone else on the planet missed out today. I actually wish I had been doing that instead of playing with lava - as crazy as that sounds.

Only later when I reflect on my day do I realize my feelings of FOMO are utter nonsense. Today was one of the best experiences of my entire life, so it's ridiculous to say I 'missed out' on anything.

I am only one person, and it's impossible to be in two places at the same time, therefore I have to choose one 'thing' at a time. As long as I always fill my time with something amazing, that is the best I can possibly do. Choosing to play with lava over sand boarding is not 'missing out' at all.

I realize 'missing out' is only about how we each feel about our own day. If we sit around and do nothing and then regret that later when friends tell us about their awesome day, then yeah, we probably 'missed out' on something. On the other hand, if we are doing something we thoroughly enjoy, and it makes us happy, we are not missing out on anything.

We are doing exactly what we should be doing.

Across Honduras

El Salvador / Honduras / Nicaragua
February 2010

D RIVING across a country in a single day is a bit of a
failure, I think. I will not try new foods, see beautiful
places or meet the locals. In short, I won't be experiencing
the country. I'm not even sure I can say I 'went' there at all.
Crossing two borders and driving three hundred miles in a
single day was not my plan from the start. The more I have
heard about Honduras, however, the more I'm certain driving
straight across in one shot is the right thing to do.

Over the last few months I have heard many horror stories
about bribery and corruption in Honduras. It seems the Police
and Military often do whatever they want to foreigners in
order to extract cash. Everyone has a different experience and
therefore a different story. My friend Rupert wound up in
handcuffs on the side of the road, narrowly avoiding a night in

jail by paying hundreds of dollars. I'm certain jail in Honduras is no fun, and I have no desire to find out for sure.

By minimizing my time in the country, I hope to lessen the chances of serious problems with the corrupt officials. I will attempt to cross Honduras in a single huge day.

El Salvador

I break camp before sunrise, then pace up and down for thirty minutes impatiently waiting for the tent fly to dry. I have it draped over the side of the Jeep to catch the morning sun, a slow but effective drying method. After a couple of hours driving in the early dawn light, I stop for gas a few miles before the Honduran border. The station attendants love the map depicting my route on the hood and we strike up a conversation, again making me appreciate how far my Spanish has come.

When I say I'm going to Honduras, both immediately look serious before explaining the most common scams. The corrupt officials will demand to see my license, then refuse to give it back unless I pay up. Knowing I will not leave without it, the officers will have me cornered and I will have little choice but to pay. It's also a certainty they will ask to see my fire extinguisher and safety triangle - the kind used on the road to warn other vehicles of a breakdown. If I fail to produce either, the corrupt Police and Military will demand a bribe with the threat of arrest or vehicle impound.

I have to smile when it turns out this very gas station sells fire extinguishers and triangles - how convenient! I start to wonder where the scams actually begin. For $16 USD I splash out and purchase both, hoping to avoid at least some conflict throughout the day. I play with my new triangle for about three seconds before I lose interest, tossing it in the back.

Even here at the gas station, a few miles before the border, fixers spot me and come running over. As usual they insist the crossing will take hours without them and only twenty minutes with. Repeatedly they say the border is extremely difficult and dangerous and I must use their help. I'm determined to stick to my guns and so I wave them away with thanks.

I pass a line of trucks stretching over two miles before I stop at a crumbling shack to cancel my El Salvadorian Jeep paperwork. I must photocopy a form and I'm not surprised to see an enterprising person has a photocopier exactly where I need it. The guy is obviously proud to charge five cents per copy - an amount he clearly thinks is exorbitant.

Fifty yards further I arrive at El Salvadorian Immigration, where nearly a hundred people are milling around. I park as conspicuously as possible, before forging ahead in an attempt to get myself stamped out. A guy wearing a uniform with ID says I must pay $3 USD to enter Honduras and will give me a somewhat-official looking receipt. I'm skeptical, believing the CA-4 stamp in my passport allows free travel between multiple countries in this region of Central America. Knowing I will spend the rest of the day arguing with people about money, I decide to let this one slide. After only a short discussion I pay the $3 USD so I can move forward quickly.

I feel certain this is only the first of many battles I will fight today.

Honduras

Men rush and literally grab onto the moving Jeep as I drive over an old crumbling bridge. They are money changers, and desperately want my business. After agreeing to a rate I change some small bills before shaking them off and inching forward. Immediately over the bridge I find myself in a dry and dusty shanty town - apparently the border post. Hundreds of grubby and exhausted people with blank expressions on their faces mill about. Almost none appear to have any purpose, simply lying still in the shade. The thermometer swinging from the rear-view mirror is maxed at 100°F, and it's only 10am.

I don't like the look of this place at all, and I feel apprehensive about leaving the Jeep unattended. After a quick look around, I ask a huge security guard holding a pump-action shotgun if he can please keep an eye on it. With a nod he puts one foot on the front bumper while scanning the crowd, shotgun at the ready across his chest.

I take that as a 'yes'.

The paperwork chase begins and I almost fall over when the Immigration guy asks for the $3 USD receipt I paid earlier - it seems that was legit and I really was supposed to pay. I'm glad I didn't argue with that guy for too long.

Before all is said and done, the following papers are shuffled, requiring multiple trips to the photocopier, bank and then back to the bank again for good measure.

- 3 copies of my passport photo page.
- 3 copies of the registration for the Jeep.
- 3 copies of my drivers license.
- 3 copies of receipt number one - 135 Lempiras ($7 USD) paid at the bank.
- 3 copies of receipt number two - 500.72 Lempiras ($26 USD) paid at the bank.
- 3 more copies of my passport, with a new Honduran entrance stamp and the $3 USD receipt from earlier.

After all the back and forth, I'm finally issued a permit for the Jeep. When I pay my Jeep guard a few dollars for his vigilance he almost shakes my hand off in thanks.

Less than a hundred yards into Honduras three Military guys eagerly wave me down. I intentionally stop in the driving lane, leave the engine running and don't get out. All three men are barely in their twenties, not yet filling out their uniforms. They are trying hard to look tough, though they all carry their assault rifles awkwardly, ruining the attempt. The oldest - clearly the leader - approaches my window.

He demands my drivers license, which he snatches away before demanding to see my fire extinguisher. I smugly produce it, still in the box and with price sticker clearly visible. Not to be deterred he immediately demands to see a safety triangle. I produce the new triangle, again still in the box, price sticker front and centre. After a quick glance he is pleased to announce I must have two triangles - one will not do.

I decide to play another angle and start replying to everything with *No entiendo* (I don't understand) in my worst-possible gringo accent. He dives into a rambling tale about how I must have two triangles for safety. I interject every sentence or two with more *No entiendo* while painting my face with a blank-trying-hard-to-understand look.

When he finally finishes, I stare blankly, with no comprehension at all. He is visibly frustrated and storms off with my license to consult his cohorts. They all frown and scowl at me while discussing the situation, clearly unsure of how to proceed. They take turns carefully inspecting my license, turning it over and holding it close to their faces. After seeing the blank backside, and how easily the card bends, the leader marches over and announces I have given him a copy. He demands the original.

I again reply many times with *No entiendo*, all the while smiling and pretending to try my absolute best to understand. He clearly knows I have given him a copy. He also knows he has nothing on me without the original. Try as he might, he is unable to make me understand he must have the original.

Ten minutes have passed since I blocked the driving lane and a transport truck is now blocking the other lane. Together we are creating a huge traffic jam and the many honks from the impatient line is too many witnesses for the inexperienced young officer. Clearly disgusted, he throws the copy of my license at me and hurries to the next customer in line.
One down, many to go.

Only a hundred yards further, I'm stopped again, this time by a friendly guy in uniform who needs to see my shiny new Honduran paperwork for the Jeep. He insists on keeping a copy for his records, which I don't have. I have three copies of the receipts and many more of all my other documents, but not a copy of the one he needs. I try hard to escape the inevitable, though he will have none of it.

With no choice I turn around, get stuck in the traffic leaving Honduras, get copies and come back. While driving past my three young Military friends I intentionally look away and have no idea if they try to stop me again. After handing over the new copy I can finally enter Honduras.

Less than three miles further a group of men in Military uniform stand from the shade of a tree and eagerly wave me down. It's abundantly clear they have been waiting for a tourist and I wonder if someone called ahead. At first I stop in the middle of the road, but they insist I park on the shoulder, so I obey. This is a game of knowing when to push my luck, and when not to. The youngest of the three - who can't be more than seventeen - approaches my window and starts with the familiar routine.

First he demands my license, followed by the fire extinguisher and triangle. I immediately produce the fire extinguisher, before really making him work to make me understand the word for triangle (*triangular* in Spanish). I say *No entiendo* so many times even I get sick of hearing it. The young officer dives into a winding tale about how a triangle is used in the event of a flat tire. I continually make it clear I have no idea what he is talking about, so to emphasise his point he kicks the nearest tire on the Jeep.

My face lights up with a huge grin as I point to the spare on the back. In the worst Spanish accent I can muster, I say: "Yes, I have five tires!"
His shoulders slump with disappointment at my obvious stupidity. Now he knows for sure - he is dealing with an imbecile.

He realizes there is no way to explain what he wants. I am simply too stupid to understand. Finally, as a last resort, he directly asks for money, begging me. Because he is so young for a split second I feel like giving it to him, though I continue with my not understanding bit. After the best puppy dog eyes he can manage, the young officer eventually gives up and waves me away.

In the mirror I see his buddies give him a hard time about returning empty handed.

This Military bribery routine is repeated twice more, in more or less similar circumstances and always with the same outcome. After wasting enough of their time and energy, I am waved through still holding all my money. Variations include a bribe because the Jeep does not have a front license plate and another officer asking if I have a jack before he hilariously pantomimes jacking up the Jeep in an attempt to make me understand. My trusty *No entiendo* response sees me through both of these and more without incident.

One stop, however, is noticeably different. The officers are not lounging in the shade, there are large barriers on the road and the entire roadblock has an official air about it. The immaculately dressed officer politely asks to see all my documentation (including Passport), asks a few quick questions about my origin and destination, then waves me through in less than thirty seconds. He even smiles and wishes me a safe journey. I gather this is an 'authorized' checkpoint, while all the others are Military guys doing whatever they want to earn extra cash, probably on their day off.

Ψ   Ψ   Ψ

The main highway is choked with painfully slow trucks and more corrupt officials, so I make a snap decision and turn East, aiming for the small border crossing at *El Espiño*. I'm immediately happy about this decision. The now excellent road winds up through small mountains, without a single

Military roadblock in sight. I pass through numerous small towns and villages that are clean and the locals seem friendly. I thoroughly enjoy this part of Honduras, and briefly consider spending the night. I keep an eagle eye out, but can't spot any hotels. With the numerous warnings about safety in Honduras, I have no intention of wild camping beside the road.

Four hours after entering Honduras, I arrive at the Nicaraguan border. The only stops have been the many Military road-blocks, official and otherwise. I'm so surprised by what I see I ask someone if this is the actual border. The whole area is spotless and quiet and not a single person hassles me. In fact, the few people I do see completely ignore me, which comes as a huge shock. This is unlike any border I have seen so far in Central America.

Still thinking it's a failure to drive across the country in one go, I want to mingle with Hondurans. With that in mind, I sit in a small roadside café for lunch, just a hundred yards before the border gates. I order tacos, and am delighted when they are hard-shelled and stuffed with cheese, onions and tomato. They are so delicious I immediately order another round, much to the delight of the lady running the busy one person operation. Striking up a conversation with locals is fun and I'm again shocked at how far my Spanish has progressed. It's great to actually reply and have a conversation rather than repeat the same three lines like a broken record. For the entire day, with the borders and bribery attempts, I have understood ninety-five percent of everything said to me. The week of intensive Spanish lessons I took in El Salvador is paying off ten-fold - making life easier and a lot more fun.

A problem arises inside the deserted Immigration office while getting stamped out of Honduras. Years ago I was granted a visitor visa for the USA and because of a mistake with the dates, it was cancelled and a replacement visa was issued immediately. Both are full pages in my passport, and the incorrect visa has a huge stamp in red, which reads 'Cancelled without Prejudice' - in English. The Immigration officer thinks this means I was kicked out or banned. He is certain anyone banned from the USA should not be allowed into Honduras. It makes no difference how many times I explain the situation, and show him my valid visa for the USA. He is determined to hold me up. Even when I point out I am already legally in Honduras and simply want to leave, he won't listen. After thirty minutes, he calls his superior to discuss what to do, and I get the feeling he wants a bribe to hurry the process along. Realizing he expects me to be in a hurry, I sit and wait patiently, making it clear I have all the time in the world.

After another thirty minutes he loses interest, gives me an exit stamp, and I'm free to go.

The attendant minding a rope across the road asks to see my Passport and papers for one last check before I can drive out of Honduras. He assures me multiple times this is absolutely the last check in Honduras, and I won't have anything else to deal with.

This really is it.

I really can leave now.

I simply must pay $10 USD, then I can go.

I politely ask for a receipt, which causes him to instantly bow his head, lower the rope and wave me through.

I can't blame the guy for trying.

Nicaragua

I have to exchange the remaining Honduran cash I have, the second time changing money today. I have absolutely no idea what the exchange rate is, having never looked it up. As usual a money changer appears just when I need him. He offers a rate I barely listen to before immediately asking for a better one. He raises it a little, and I apply a little more pressure. Twice more he raises the rate before turning to walk away, saying that's the best he can do.

OK, I say, I'll take that.

After a clean, quiet and easy border crossing I drive into the streets of Nicaragua in the late afternoon, country number three for the day.

I will be the first to admit I've picked up horrendous driving habits since crossing into Mexico many months ago. Road rules simply do not apply here - more often than not it's safer to ignore them anyway. I honestly have not looked at a speed limit in months, I couldn't care less for give way or stop signs, and I completely ignore double lines on the road. Red lights I do mostly obey, except when it's easier to flow with the moving traffic and just go through.

Extremely slow vehicles and horse-drawn carts are common occurrences in Central America, and in my usual style I zip around one on the outside of a blind corner. I cross double lines, doing about 50 mph, nothing unusual. Two Policemen are waiting at the bottom of the hill, and eagerly flag me down. I once again get the feeling they were waiting for me, having been tipped off to my approach.

After taking my license it becomes clear they will write a ticket for my many infractions. It will be about a $20 USD ticket, they tell me. The catch is they will hold onto my license while I pay at a nearby bank. I was clearly breaking the law and caught red handed, so I'm happy to pay the legitimate fine. The problem comes when I must back-track a long way to a specific bank. They only have a copy of my license, which I could easily abandon, but with no other way around I can't drive away from the bank. By making me back-track, the officers have ensured I must pass by them after visiting the bank.

During this lengthy negotiation, the sun has inched below the horizon. My one and only golden rule is to avoid driving in the dark at all costs due to the serious dangers present on the roads at night. After talking around the problem it becomes clear they need money for gas, so I give them 100 *Córdobas* ($5 USD), literally everything I have in my wallet.

Immediately, the two Policemen are my best friends. The ticket is forgotten, my license is returned and they helpfully give directions to my destination before wishing me well.
Only the second speeding ticket of my life, and I bribed my way out of it - nice!

As I pull away from the waving officers, it dawns on me maybe Nicaragua is stricter with road rules. Maybe I should toe the line more than I have been lately if I want to avoid more tickets.
These good intentions last all of five minutes before I fall back to my old ways of driving as I please.

I drive through an endless dusk before the light fades entirely and I find myself in pitch black. Having never once driven in the dark since entering Mexico, I find it difficult and intimidating. Horses, bicycles, children, abandoned vehicles, pot holes and farm equipment materialize out of the darkness, and I work overtime on concentration.
Now I remember why I don't drive at night.

Hours later I pull into a large gas station and feel an overwhelming sense of déjà-vu. The entire place is spotless inside and out. Shelves are stacked with the requisite junk food and a line of people wait at the attached fast food joint. The top 100 music playing in English helps complete the picture.

Finally, at 9:30pm, I climb stiffly out of the Jeep, safely parked in front of the Big Foot hostel in downtown *Leòn*.
I have driven 320 miles across three countries in fourteen and a half hours.
We did it.
Good Jeep.

After a cold shower and one beer, I fall into a dreamless sleep.

A Gap In The Road

Panama and Colombia
March 2010

D RIVING the entire Pan-American Highway from Alaska
to Argentina has one small problem - there is no road
between Panama and Colombia, just sixty miles of dense jungle
and swamp, called The Darien Gap.

A couple of seriously well-equipped vehicles have technically
driven it, so the Guinness Book of Records is correct in listing
the Pan-Am as the longest drivable road in the world. The
first vehicle ever to do it - a Jeep - took over seven hundred
days. Yes, that's right, two years to drive sixty miles. It's not
something I'm interested in attempting.

Rumors suggest the current President of Panama is interested
in building the highway through to Colombia, and Brazil have
offered to fund construction. The topic is debated every few
years, with a lot of opposition due to political, environmental

and economic concerns. Everyone agrees the USA will never allow construction to begin because a highway to South America is seen as a boom for the drug trade. I'm not holding my breath for construction to start any time soon.

Besides the two year jungle slog or waiting for a road to be built, there are a few ways to cross The Gap with a vehicle:

- Load the car into a standard shipping container and use traditional ocean freight, normally from the port of *Colón* in Panama to *Cartegena* in Colombia. Costs are roughly $1000 USD per vehicle.
- Roll-On, Roll-Off (RORO) services, which are similar to a ferry. The main difference is the port workers have the keys and drive the vehicle at each end. This method appears to be relatively cheap, in the $500 USD range, though it is accompanied by many horror stories of theft of everything inside the vehicle.
- Lift-On, Lift-Off (LOLO) services, where the vehicle is lifted with a crane on and off the ship, without handing over the keys. This is the only choice for large vehicles that don't fit inside a shipping container. This option is expensive, quickly climbing well over $2000 USD for a big camper.
- The motorbike guys have a huge advantage here and can transport their bikes on small pleasure yachts. Riders can travel with their bikes, and spend a week sailing through the beautiful white sand beaches of the *San Blas Islands*. Costs are around $700 USD for bike and rider.

At times a traditional ferry has made the crossing, though it went bankrupt a few years ago. It seems the powers-that-be continue to undermine attempts to start a new one and won't issue the required permits.

Since meeting Rupert and Amy months ago at the Belize/Guatemala border, crossing The Gap has been in the back of my mind. After bumping into multiple people on the road, I join a huge email chain of other overlanders travelling the Americas. I get to know a French couple literally only a week behind me, also moving South. Vince and Marie are a few years into their around the world adventure in their Land Rover and are looking to share a forty foot shipping container, big enough for both vehicles. Sharing makes the crossing cheaper for everyone. More than saving money, it's great to team up with other overlanders I relate to so well. From the minute we meet, Vince and Marie fill my head with stories of grand adventures on a global scale.

Quickly I must learn a lot of new terminology related to the shipping industry. In his prior life as an Engineer Vince was heavily involved with shipping and therefore understands the complicated process. He explains the key to a successful transit is to obsess over the tiny details. We must negotiate exactly what is included in the price, otherwise a ton of 'extras' will bite us later.

For example, it's possible we could pay extra for the container to be moved to a location suitable for loading, we could pay extra to have the vehicles 'lashed' down and we could pay extra simply to open the door of the container.
As I understand it, we could be forced to pay extra for pretty much anything.

The following terminology quickly becomes part of my world:

- **Ocean Freight:** The cost of actually shipping the container from port A to port B.
- **Bunker:** The cost of fuel for the ship.
- **Stuffing:** Getting the vehicles into the container and sealing it. The details here are important as this may include moving the container from the port to a yard or not.
- **Lashing:** Physically securing the vehicles into the container so they don't move.
- **Un-stuffing:** Opening the container and getting the vehicles out. Again this may include moving the container around or not.

- **Documentation Fee:** The cost of creating and then submitting the required Customs paperwork.
- **Bill of Lading:** The most important document, describing the contents of the container, and importantly who owns it.
- **Port Fees:** The amount charged by the port to allow the container and it's contents to pass through.

All of the above may be charged per container or per vehicle, and may cover one or both ports. I quickly learn shipping is a shady operation where everyone wants a slice of the pie and will invent fees or change the rules of the game any way they please.

Day 1 - Finding a Shipping Company

Driving and navigating in Panama City is utterly nuts, so we leave the vehicles at our hostel and take cheap taxis around the city, an adventure in itself. The city drivers are basically suicidal, always driving at breakneck speeds with complete disregard for their own safety. Most taxis in the city are literally falling apart, much worse than anything I have ever seen. Often there are no seat belts, lights or door handles and sometimes not even a windshield. I become seriously impressed at the drivers' ability to jam cars into spaces they simply shouldn't fit. Despite the madness surrounding me, I don't see a single accident.

To add to the excitement, taxi prices must be strictly negotiated before we climb in, otherwise we will be stuck with a huge bill at our destination. Often when we ask, the driver will name a price that is three or four times higher than the price we are able to finally negotiate. These negotiations can turn into a tense standoff, with drivers refusing our low-ball offers and moving away, only to immediately reverse and accept. We are told this heavy negotiating earns respect in the eyes of locals, because it's part of life in Panama. Anyone that doesn't negotiate on prices deserves to be separated from their money. From riding in taxis and buying lunch to shipping agents and street vendors, negotiating is life in Panama City.

The intense heat and humidity mean I'm bathed in sweat from the minute I wake until taking a cold shower in the evening and I finish my half-gallon water bottle before 10am. This weather is energy-sapping, and combined with endless negotiations in Spanish I'm physically and mentally exhausted by midday.

Seaboard Marine Shipping Line are the well known favorite of overlanders and offer a good service for a reasonable price. Before we even explain ourselves, we're handed a pre-prepared quote. Clearly the only foreigners who walk through the door are looking to ship vehicles to Colombia. The $1880 USD quote appears comprehensive. It is for two vehicles and lists all the various line items Vince warned about earlier. However, we find it confusing un-stuffing is per vehicle, which is never adequately explained to us. Of course, none of this is supposed to make sense. After much discussion and negotiation Seaboard will not budge even one dollar on their quote. It is what it is, take it or leave it.
We decide to move on, using this as our baseline.

Barwil Shipping Line are the second favorite of overlanders and again clearly deal with foreigners regularly - a friendly lady speaking perfect English ushers us into a pristine air-conditioned office. I immediately feel comfortable and relaxed, and wonder if that's by design. The basic quote we are handed is comprised of a single line on a single page. At $1900 USD it's in the ballpark, though unfortunately there is no cost breakdown. Attempting to clarify, we are told everything is included except Customs charges in Colombia, something that is out of their hands. We are assured these charges "will not be more than $200 - $400 USD per vehicle," which is not at all reassuring.

Again the quote is a good starting point, though we are determined to find a cheaper way to get our vehicles to Colombia. Vince loves to wheel and deal, and is not happy with these non-negotiable quotes clearly prepared for foreigners. He is certain they contain a healthy profit for the shipping line and we should be able to do better. While waiting in the Barwil office, Marie picks up a newspaper dedicated to ocean freight that lists many shipping lines in Panama City we have never heard of. We feel encouraged contacting them and hope there will even be room for negotiation - just like everything else in Panama City.

Marfret (Rozo) Shipping Line is one company listed in the shipping newspaper. Partly as a joke, Vince and Marie get in touch because it's a French company. Soon after walking through the door, we meet Raiza, a friendly assistant. Unfortunately neither Raiza nor anyone else in the office actually speaks French and so we once again negotiate in Spanish. After a lengthy wait we are given a quote of $1460 USD - much lower than the competition. It's so low we are not sure if it's complete or even represents what we want. Attempting to clarify the details with Raiza, it is obvious she doesn't know the details and doesn't want to commit to anything.

We leave the office with more questions than before we arrived, though we are excited about the possibility of a much cheaper option.

Back at our hostel we conclude Seaboard Marine's comprehensive quote is in the lead, and will continue to investigate the options at Marfret and several other companies we have contacted.

Day 2 - The Search Continues

While taxing around town investigating more options, we receive an email from Marfret. Unfortunately, the email does not directly answer any of our questions and we find ourselves even less certain about what the quote does and does not include. Desperately needing answers, we take a taxi directly to the office. Again Raiza is unable to answer our questions with certainty, though she mentions her boss will be in the office shortly should we wish to speak with him.

When Mr. Martinez arrives everything immediately changes. He is extremely professional, speaks excellent English and clarifies every question we have and then some. He even reduces the original quote because un-stuffing is per container, not per vehicle - exactly what we had been thinking. The quote is now down to $1233 USD and our confidence this can work is growing by the minute. That lasts all of two minutes before Mr. Martinez mentions we have just one hurdle remaining.

Marfret is purely a shipping line - they don't handle any of the complicated paperwork required.
For that we need a Customs broker.

On the recommendation of Mr. Martinez we race across town to the office of Mario, a specialty Customs broker. Mario's eyes constantly dart around as he speaks rapidly in what we think is broken Spanish. His cheap suit and cramped office in a nondescript high rise have me thinking of private detectives in B-grade movies. I get the impression Mario sees us as walking bags of money.

After clarifying exactly what we need, Mario explains in great detail the process is long and difficult. Because of the huge amount of time he will spend on this, his price is $250 USD per vehicle. With a French/Spanish mix, Vince jumps in and takes the lead in a lengthy negotiation. Over the course of a rambling story Vince explains this high price combined with Marfret's quote pushes the total higher than other shipping lines. We thank Mario for his services and begin to leave, when suddenly Mario drops his price to $100 USD per vehicle. Not yet content, Vince pushes harder and manages to negotiate for Mario to provide a fixer to guide us through the difficult process ahead. Vince is clearly proud of his negotiating skills, and I'm extremely impressed he was able to get this deal. Maybe this goes against my 'no fixers' rule, but Mario threw it in free and I'm happy for all the help we can get.

We aim to sail on Sunday, so we must seal the vehicles in the container on Friday, leaving not a single day to spare. We'll make it.

We hope.

Day 3 - Customs, Inspections & Insanity

The first order of business in the long and complicated paperwork process is to ask permission from Customs to take our temporarily imported vehicles out of Panama. This is not straightforward because we are not leaving the country with our vehicles. While they will sail on a container ship, we must fly in a regular passenger plane and meet them in Colombia.

Our first stop is a Police compound where our vehicles must be inspected to verify they match the documentation given to us when entering Panama. Inspections are only performed from 10-11am, so we arrive at 9:30, eager to get the ball rolling. Waiting in the parking lot becomes amusing when another two French couples with vehicles show up, and then four other foreign guys on motorbikes.

A polite Policeman warns us this is an unsafe neighborhood and we should be extra vigilant. He insists we must be especially cautious of the many children milling about, who will quickly snatch anything left unattended. This is all baffling given we are standing in the parking lot of a Police station, though it's abundantly clear the officer is not joking. We all keep a careful eye on our stuff, and never leave the vehicles unattended, even for a second. Mario's fixer eventually arrives, and immediately sets about lounging in the shade.

When my turn comes, I wait anxiously as the senior inspector glances at the VIN of the Jeep. In one second he circles a problem on my paperwork before shoving the papers back and silently walking away. A junior officer explains the VIN is correct, but at the border only the first half was listed under 'Engine Number', which is not acceptable. My Jeep doesn't have an Engine Number, and he says the complete VIN must be listed there. With the incorrect paperwork, I will not be permitted to ship the Jeep out of Panama. It must be corrected at all costs. Suddenly, our Sunday sailing feels extremely soon.

With not a second to spare, I jump in the Jeep with Mario's fixer and together we race to the head office of Customs. I feel overwhelmed when I see an enormous line of people trying to get Customs paperwork approved. Mario's fixer springs into action, and for a small fee I am able to skip the line. I'm soon issued a new temporary import permit - this time with the complete VIN listed under Engine Number. We race back to get the Jeep re-inspected, and thankfully the new paperwork is approved by the grumpy senior inspector.

Relief washes over me, but only lasts two minutes before Mario's fixer runs over waving his arms. A problem has been found with Vince's paperwork. After being told his paperwork was complete and correct, Vince left it at the office. Seeing no point in waiting for me, Vince and Marie have returned to the hostel, and are now unaware of any problem. Because we're sharing a container, Vince's paperwork problem is my paperwork problem.

Clutching Vince's paperwork, I race back to the Customs head office. After practicing on a scrap of paper I sweat while forging Vince's signature on the new paperwork. Nobody seems to notice, and I get away with it. Back at the inspection yard I submit Vince's new paperwork, barely making the cut-off.

While rushing back and forward I bump into the other French overlanders and two of the motorbike guys on the same run around. They also have stupid mistakes on their paperwork and are frantically trying to correct them. We each pay $10 USD to skip the line and pay for our corrected forms. I start to wonder if this is a game cooked up by Customs to extract money from us.

Ψ   Ψ   Ψ

Later the same afternoon a different Police office opens, where we must have our paperwork approved and signed-off. Mario said our Customs fixer would meet us there, and so we wait for him before entering the building.
Thinking we need his help, we wait and wait.

Stress levels slowly rise as we watch multiple people frantically run from the building to make a photocopy of some random form. Everyone needs a different set of copies - there appears to be no rhyme or reason to this madness. After calling twice our guy finally shows, and we're ready to get started. Immediately we hit a hurdle when the security guard won't let us enter wearing shorts or flip-flops. This is not negotiable.

After we shuffle and borrow clothes and shoes from anyone we can, everyone makes it inside - everyone except me. The plan is for me to wear Vince's borrowed clothes when he is finished, though with time quickly running out, I realize I won't make it. In desperation, I resort to begging everyone around the office. After completing his paperwork, one of the kind motorbike guys lends me his pants and boots while he wears my shorts and flip-flops. I'm finally permitted to enter the office at 4:57pm, just as the lady behind the desk announces she will not process anymore paperwork today.

Pleading does the trick, and the paperwork chase begins in earnest. At one point I hold three identical copies of each of my eight pieces of paper. Every single piece of paper has at least three stamps and an equal number of signatures.
Why all of this is necessary, I have no idea.

Miraculously, I scrape through and am given a single piece of paper that for an unknown reason has become the focus of my life. With it, I should be good to go.

A problem has been found with the paperwork of the other overlanders, so everything grinds to a halt for them. The inspection office is now closed for the day, so nothing can be done until 10am tomorrow, when they can start the entire process over again.

This couple are also short on time and have already booked non-refundable plane tickets to Colombia. Their well laid plans are quickly falling apart. Stress levels and exhaustion are through the roof for everybody, though mostly for this French couple who can not progress. We all understand when he completely loses it, yelling and screaming at everyone in ear shot. This, of course, does not help anything.

Somehow, Vince and I have passed the tests and have survived to progress another day.

We are a step closer to Colombia and South America. The madness and excitement continue to build.

Day 4 - Stuffing

The big day has arrived. Today we 'stuff' our vehicles into the container, which has us buzzing with excitement. Driving in rush hour traffic with horns honking and tires squealing is better than a wake up coffee. Our first stop is Mario's office for last minute paperwork and payment. We would prefer to pay after the job is done, though we don't have any say in the matter. Unhappy with this situation, we mention his fixer 'bribed' us $20 USD to get our forms corrected at Customs, which kicks off a massive argument. Vince yells in a French/Spanish mix, causing Mario to rise to the challenge and yell back just as loudly. Both men stand and wave their arms wildly while ranting and raving, while I only catch the odd word here and there.

Finally, completely fed up, Mario throws our stack of paperwork and says we can do it without him for all he cares. Vince's fast talking pays off again, and he soon smooths over the situation. He is able to calm Mario, and get things back on track.

Mario needs another hour and we think it best to let him cool off, so we disappear and leave him to it.

Hoping to avoid exorbitant charges in Colombia we want to thoroughly clean the vehicles. When the container is opened in Colombia, they will be thoroughly inspected by port officials. Even the smallest trace of mud can cause the whole process to be delayed, or worse still, Customs can charge astronomical fees for subsequent cleaning and fumigation.

After having the vehicles pressure washed until we can eat off the undercarriage, we return to Mario's office and are amazed to find everything is ready. We even persuade Mario to send his fixer with us to the port, who makes no attempt to hide his dislike of this agreement. The fixer jumps into his transit van and drives through the city like a maniac, not once waiting for us. We do our best to keep up as we merge onto the frantic freeway to *Colón*, before settling in for the sixty mile journey. In *Colón* it's easy to find the port - it is so enormous we see it long before arriving in the city.

Driving into the port I feel like we have stumbled into a giant labyrinth. Built with tens of thousands of shipping containers stacked impossibly high, the maze makes me feel like a mouse in an experiment. Soon I'm disoriented and become hopelessly lost as we make turn after turn, always deeper into the maze.

We are given more copies to add to our collection and more important looking-stamps at the Marfret office. What purpose they serve, I have no idea. Our fixer walks us to the 'free-zone' and the huge Customs compound within. Here we hand over the huge stack of papers we have collected so far and receive a permit for our vehicles to legally exit the country. Again every piece of paper is completed in triplicate, including stamps and signatures. I smile broadly as the stamp in my passport preventing me leaving Panama is also cancelled.

Amazingly, we bump into the French overlanders once again, who miraculously talked around their paperwork problem and are back in the game. It's clear the stress has taken a toll - they had a sleepless night and look five years older than just yesterday.

Back at the port a man calls us into an office to issue security passes. He explains in great detail where we must take the vehicles, which sounds easy enough. Now clutching our new security passes, the fixer tells us to stand in a huge line of people where we must hand over our paperwork. Saying we are essentially finished, he bids us farewell, never to be seen again.

Time is rapidly running out and we begin to feel anxious about the port closing time. Forty-five minutes after handing over our precious paperwork we're still waiting in the scorching sun. We summarize our position as such:

- We have no idea why we are standing in line.
- We have no idea why we gave all our paperwork away.
- We have no idea why we must pay $5 USD each.
- We hope like mad we are in the right place doing the right thing.

When our huge stack of papers is eventually returned we drive clear across the port. We are extremely excited to actually load the container, which we naively assume will happen shortly.

The directions given earlier are more confusing than helpful, and we find ourselves driving aimlessly around the massive port with no clue where to go. Searching frantically we even drive up and down a muddy gravel road, negating our clean vehicle plan from earlier. Completely stuck as to where to go next, Vince stops at a security checkpoint to ask directions. The armed men furiously yell and wave their arms before he can even speak, so we quickly reverse, abandoning that plan.

We see a group of people milling about a temporary building clutching paperwork and realize we must look the same. We reason even if it's not the correct place, hopefully they can give directions. With no better option, we attempt to walk into the fenced yard surrounding the office. An armed guard blocks our way, demanding we hand over our passports. In return for leaving them at the gate, we are issued yet another security badge.

It soon becomes clear we are at the extremely busy RORO section of the port where locals are furiously importing vehicles into Panama. In a huge line I see everything from sports cars to tractors, trucks and motorbikes. Many have severe damage, though everyone is excited about getting them into the country. We still have no idea if we're in the right place, so we ask the lady in the office. Without reply she takes half of our paperwork before giving the other half to a man standing around who simply says "Wait here."
And so we do.

At this point Vince and I are both exhausted and seriously doubt we are in the correct place. We do not feel good about this. To add to our woes, we just gave away all the paperwork that has become the focus of our lives.

With little choice, we mill around in the hot sun feeling lost and helpless, just like everyone else. Heat, exhaustion and frustration make losing it look like a valid option at this point. If I had the energy, I would do just that.

After what feels like an eternity we get an indication of progress when the guards who yelled and waved furiously earlier say we can enter their compound. Now friendly, they let us drive into the yard for a K-9 inspection. Ten minutes later a huge German Shepherd climbs in and on everything in the Jeep before moving to Vince's Land Rover. He never once looks anything other than downright bored.

Again we wait, nervously watching as 4:30pm comes and goes. We are hyper aware the port closes at 5pm sharp.

Finally, a Customs officer wanders over and says he can take us to our container. We both smile from ear to ear, and for the first time I feel like we might just pull this off. We eagerly drive deep into the massive port, past row after row of shipping containers stacked precariously high.

I have never been inside a major shipping port like this, and I'm stunned. Even with my exhaustion I can not help but be in awe of the scale. We drive to within twenty yards of the water, where cargo ships the size of small cities glide slowly and silently past. Directly overhead a crane too big to be real whips back and forward, slinging containers onto huge piles.

I park in front of a lone shipping container sitting with the door open. Relief washes over us when we realize we have actually made it, and we smile and joke at our success against all odds. We feel as if nothing can stop us now.

Both vehicles have another K-9 inspection before the dog walks one lap around the empty container, thoroughly checking each corner. We intentionally ordered a forty foot 'high cube' container so Vince can drive straight in with his tall roof top tent attached. He slowly inches in while I stand on the rear bumper to watch for clearance - it's close, but it fits. After Vince climbs out his window, I park directly behind the Land Rover. I intentionally park a fraction closer to one side, leaving just enough space for me to squeeze out the driver's door.

While waiting for the lashing crew I sit quietly on the concrete at 4:50pm, feeling jubilant and exhausted at the same time. While taking photos of the Jeep inside the container, I sneak a photo of the huge port before an officer tells me photos are not permitted. All four wheels of both vehicles are chocked with timber, and the four corners are tied down with rope, tight enough to compress the suspension and solidly enough to satisfy us. Vince and I conduct a quick inspection and take a few photos inside the container before we sign yet more forms. A Customs officer closes the heavy door and attaches a special seal. This is an International seal that must be intact upon arrival in Colombia to prove the container and it's contents have not been tampered with.

Now there is nothing more for us to do.

We walk the length of the port, exchanging security badges for passports as we go. At 5:30pm I sit on the gutter to eat my 'lunch' of fried chicken, fries and a coke, the first thing I have eaten since 7am. I'm shaking with hunger and exhaustion, though also extremely happy with our achievement.

We catch a taxi into downtown *Colón*, aiming for the bus depot. The taxi driver warns us this is not a safe place, and insists we wait in the taxi until the bus arrives so we can get on directly. I doze for the hour ride back to the bus terminal in Panama City before we catch one last taxi to our hostel.

This has been by far the biggest, most insane few days of paperwork of my entire life. As I drift off to sleep I can't help smiling at the enormity of it all.

20,000 miles, nine months and ten countries complete, the journey continues to grow.

A new continent awaits.

Day 5 - Payment and plane tickets

Again we're moving before the sun, going to the Marfret office for the last time to settle our bill. Vince explains it's standard practice in the shipping industry to wait until the container is loaded before paying. Marfret are not worried about us not paying because they have the original Bill of Lading, without which we have no claim to the container and it's precious contents. After payment Marfret will hand over the original Bill Of Lading which we will use to claim ownership of the vehicles. We're guaranteed to pay, and Marfret knows it.

We've been working with many different versions of the quote, with each one showing slightly different line items. Complex calculations are made while we wait, and we're both stunned when the final figure is significantly lower than expected. We each pay $554 USD without saying a word.

Vince and Marie are able to buy plane tickets online, though for whatever reason my credit card is not accepted. I hope I can purchase a ticket directly from the airline, so I jump into a taxi and venture into the heart of the city alone. My card is still not accepted, so the friendly lady gives directions to the nearest ATM. Walking through the heart of bustling Panama City is great fun, and I even stop to buy street food for lunch. I don't enjoy it nearly so much walking back with a wad of US cash in my pocket. Once my ticket is paid for, I can finally relax.

Our flight is not until tomorrow evening, so I enjoy the much needed rest.

Day 6 - Panama to Colombia

The airport is far outside the city, and to save money we want to catch a public bus. We hike to where we think the bus stops and set about waiting impatiently. The sun beats down relentlessly and after almost an hour with no bus we begin to worry about missing our flight. Uncertain of what to do, we catch a taxi to the main bus depot and easily locate the correct bus. Sitting empty, we get the entire back seat, perfect for us and our bags.

When we finally get underway we're amused after twenty minutes when the bus stops where we had been waiting earlier. It seems we really were in the right place after all. As we drive through the city more and more people board, until every seat and even the aisle is full. On and on we travel, and amazingly people continue to board the bus until every square inch is jammed. The humidity inside is more intense than anything I have ever experienced, so soon everyone is drenched in sweat. I'm stunned looking at the faces of the other passengers. They are clearly city workers who make this commute daily, and all are completely exhausted and dead to the world around them. Though the city promises higher paying jobs, I have to wonder if the trade-off is worth it. This multi-hour commute is brutal.

Traffic is slow, causing us to nervously glance at our watches and ask other passengers if we have missed our stop.

"It is further."

"Keep waiting," we are told.

With the aisle completely blocked I start to wonder how we will exit the bus when the time comes. Without a word a smiling young man opens the rear emergency exit and helps us climb down before passing down our bags. The bus chugs away in a cloud of black smoke and we find ourselves on the side of the highway, half a mile from the International airport. It feels odd walking to such a massive airport, a first for me. The clean, bright and air-conditioned airport could easily be anywhere in the world.

After an easy one hour flight we land in *Cartegena* and step onto the runway into even more intense humidity. After clearing Immigration and Customs we catch a taxi to a cheap hotel downtown. It's just after 2am when my head hits the pillow for my first night in South America.

I fall asleep almost instantly.

Day 7 - Cartegena, Colombia

In the morning we move to an even cheaper hotel, not far from the port in *Cartegena*. It's another blisteringly hot and humid day as we walk to see our Customs Agent, hoping to get a head start on the paperwork game. The port of *Cartegena* is infamous for delays and the kind of bureaucracy I have come to love in Latin America. There are all manner of horror stories from paying many hundreds of dollars in bribes, to vehicles being impounded without explanation. I fully expect retrieving our vehicles from the container will be more difficult than putting them inside in Panama.

The Marfret agent knows all about us and miraculously has paperwork ready and waiting. Again there are multiple copies, stamps and signatures, which if anything is even more official and serious than in Panama. The agent wants $35 USD each for a 'Documentation Fee', which we immediately try to talk our way out of. When the agent sees the original quote that includes a $50 USD fee, he happily raises the fee to $50 USD.

After a good deal of negotiating we end up paying $35 USD each and split the other $15 USD. Again we have absolutely no idea why, and again conclude it's not supposed to make sense. We pay the money and move on, still feeling good about our overall costs due to the unexpectedly low price paid in Panama.
One hurdle down, many to go.

At the port entrance is a huge Customs building where we again bump into our French friends. It's great to see familiar faces and we catch up on developments since we last saw them. Inside I'm impressed when a Customs officer finds our container in a database and immediately knows when the ship docked, when our container was offloaded and exactly where it's sitting within the port.

After filling out a temporary import permit for the vehicles and making certain we have exactly the right number of copies, we wait while everything is typed up. The office is extremely professional, clean and air conditioned and I'm happy with how quickly things move along. With things moving so smoothly it's really only a matter of time until something stops us - and that something is lunch. There is a mandatory two hour *siesta* in Colombia, so we settle in for more waiting.

After *siesta* we're told the only person who can sign our final paperwork is in a meeting, so we settle in to wait, yet again. Another two hours later we finally get the last signature and can now collect the container. Inside the port we're issued security passes and meet a man that has been waiting for us. He speaks great English and obviously assists tourists through this process regularly, which makes everything much easier for us.

Without life insurance, I will not be permitted to enter the actual port, which means I can not drive the Jeep out myself. As much as I want to go in, I know it's not worth the hassle. I give the keys to Vince so we can keep the process moving as quickly as possible. Amazingly, safety appears to be an actual consideration here - something I have not seen for many months. The port workers check Vince's insurance before issuing him a hi-vis vest and hardhat. I can already see things in Colombia are much different than Central America.

The plan is set. Vince will drive the two vehicles out of the container and park them on the concrete. Because they will be 'stored' in the port, we must pay for storage. They will sit for literally three minutes, but that's technically storage which must be paid for. Miraculously we are not selected for a 'random' Customs inspection, so we avoid more fees and delays. After completing still more paperwork, more checking and more clearances I watch Vince drive the Jeep out of the port and park right in front of me. With a huge gin he returns to collect his Land Rover.

Retrieving a vehicle from this port in a single day is virtually unheard of. My research suggested we could pay hundreds in inspection and Customs fees and wait days for the process to run it's course. Talk about a lucky break.

At 9:15pm I drive onto the streets of *Cartagena*, elated to be driving my Jeep in South America.
I'm pinching myself and can't believe this is the Jeep I drove to Alaska and now I'm driving it in South America.

An entirely new continent lays ahead of me.

On Going Solo

W HEN I first dreamed of this journey and decided to post stories and photos on my website, I also wanted to capture my feelings and emotions along the way. I planned to write about the good times as well as the bad. I felt it was important to paint an accurate picture of solo life on the road and my state of mind along the way.

Here goes.

Ψ   Ψ   Ψ

As my dreams took shape and I became determined to make the trip, I threw myself into saving money and planning. I knew the trip would be a lot more fun with a co-pilot and so occasionally I mentioned my plans to friends and other adventurous people I met in the Canadian Rockies.

Virtually everyone I talked to thought I was nuts.

Firstly, there were the many safety concerns. Secondly, the perceived logistical barriers. After conducting no research of their own, many people declare such an undertaking too dangerous and impossible. It's as if their response was pre-programmed, deeply ingrained from years of watching the news. Even when I pointed out that many people have successfully completed an expedition through the Americas, they refused to engage their brain. It seems many people would rather believe what they believe than seek out new information.

On the very rare occasion I met someone who might be interested in joining me, they quickly declared the trip financially impossible. Everyone has a cell phone contract and bills to pay. Most people also have huge car payments and student loans. When a few other expenses are tacked on, savings accounts are unheard of. Financially, I never met anyone who could afford a couple of years off full-time work.

Added to this, many people worry about their career, and what would happen if they dropped off the map for a couple of years. For many taking two years off full-time work is literally impossible.

And so the list of potential co-pilots was exactly zero, which left me with a choice to make.

I could give up my dream and not go, or I could hit the road solo.

Ψ   Ψ   Ψ

There are many obvious advantages to making the journey with two (or more) people. As the months turned into years, I flip-flopped back and forth. Sometimes I loved the freedom of being solo, and sometimes I struggled, wishing for a team-mate.

One big plus of going in a team is the constant companionship. Having a team-mate (or two) means there will always be someone to bounce ideas off, to share the hard times and of course to enjoy the best times.

I had friends like Duke and Kate join the trip, which was a fantastic way to break things up. There were also many backpackers who jumped aboard for everything from a few hours to a few weeks. These people helped fill that need, though it was far from constant.

Of course, being part of a team also means it's possible to get more done, because the team can divide and conquer. One person can visit Immigration while the other visits Customs. One can pickup groceries while one buys gas. The first time I realized Marie was making sandwiches while Vince drove I was blown-away.
Being more efficient is a huge plus, because it means less time is spent on annoying jobs, and more is spent on enjoyment.

Without a doubt, there are also safety advantages. If presented with a bad situation, more people is almost always better. It's also really nice to have one person stay to keep an eye on the vehicle while the other is running errands.

Finally, going with two people makes the expedition more affordable. Each person contributes their savings, though many expenses are the same for one or two people - expenses like gas and shipping the vehicle across continents. Each person therefore will pay less for the expedition than if they were solo.

$$\Psi \quad \Psi \quad \Psi$$

Contrary to what you might think, there are also some advantages to going solo.

With nobody to talk to in English day-to-day, I was forced to learn Spanish, and learn it fast. In the most basic way, I had to learn to communicate with locals if I wanted human interaction. At first it seemed beyond me. I have never seriously tried to learn a language before, and honestly didn't know if I could. In High School I barely learned how to count to ten and the days of the week in a couple of languages, which was apparently enough for good marks. The idea of a conversation in another language always felt impossibly hard. I had serious doubts my Engineer-trained brain had the ability to learn a language.

During the early days, friendly Mexicans would try to strike up a conversation on the street or in a bar. Soon it became clear I could barely understand the basics, so they would excuse themselves politely and move on. This motivated me to work harder than ever before, and little-by-little my Spanish improved. By talking to the attendants at gas stations, vendors in street markets and anyone else who would put up with my terrible pronunciation, I slowly gained confidence. A week of intensive lessons in El Salvador also helped immensely.

Learning Spanish is a life achievement I am extremely proud of. My trip was much more rewarding because I was able to join random conversations and learn about life in Latin America from locals. Not speaking English every day and being alone gave me the kick I needed to focus on learning, and I'm not sure if it would have happened if there was always an English-speaker in the passenger seat.

I also quickly learned my interactions with locals were much more intense when I was alone. When Duke or Kate or anyone else was with me, I sensed locals were less likely to approach and start chatting. When locals see two people they assume they are fine and don't need anything, making them much less likely to approach and start a conversation. This changes interactions with locals.

When I was alone I had nobody to talk to - an open invitation for a chat. I found locals much more likely to strike up a conversation, and even offer assistance.

Also, being alone for so many hours in the Jeep gave me plenty of time for reflection and thought, an activity I thoroughly enjoy. Something about my personality needs plenty of this each day to keep my thoughts in order, so I was never unhappy driving alone.

So it would not be accurate to say there are no advantages to going solo.

Ψ   Ψ   Ψ

Of course, there are disadvantages to going solo too. Over time, I learned to mitigate - but never completely eliminate - the two main disadvantages I experienced.

Loneliness became the biggest one for me, and was never far from my mind in the second half of the trip. I eventually found a solution which worked well enough.

Whenever I felt overly lonely, I would search out the biggest nearby hostel. All throughout Central and South America they are packed with foreign backpackers having the time of their lives. Staying a night or two meant I could grab a beer and meet new and interesting travellers while relaxing and speaking English. More than a few times backpackers I met this way jumped in the Jeep, providing instant companionship.

Even when meeting new people, however, I felt like none of them actually *knew* me. As a traveller the same questions play out each day - where are you from, where are you going, how long are you traveling.

These are always filler conversations that just barely skim the surface. Because they are between two people that are essentially strangers, the conversations are rarely important. This meant nobody around me actually knew *who* I am, so they were unable to help when I was having a bad day or feeling lost.

So stopping at an English-speaking hostel helped, though it certainly did not completely solve my feelings of loneliness.

The second big disadvantage of going solo for me was a feeling that what I was doing had no purpose, because I was always

alone. One of Chris McCandless' greatest lessons is "Happiness is only real when shared" - something I have spent hours pondering. I certainly struggled doing so many activities and having all these experiences alone.
What's the point?, I often thought to myself.

A few times while talking to someone I just met, I would start a sentence with "Hey, remember those mountains in Colombia..?", before realizing they had not been there. In fact, nobody else was there. In a sense, many of my experiences feel less real because I have nobody to remember them with, even to this day.

As strange as it sounds, posting to my website helped with his one. I originally thought my website would be just a diary and photo album - a record of what I did each day. My friends and family might be interested in the photos, and it would be a great way to keep a permanent record of the trip - for *me*.

I had no idea people I have never met would comment and encourage me so frequently. The same familiar people would repeatedly comment, and I started to have a real sense they knew who I was. They knew what I liked and disliked, they could even tell when I had had a bad day. Although we never met, having their support and knowing they were 'with' me was a huge help. More than once the knowledge people were following provided the motivation to keep going.

Sharing my experiences on my website, and knowing people were following along helped make many experiences more real in my mind. Doing so greatly helped to reduce the feeling that what I was doing was pointless.

So going solo is not ideal, though it certainly has a couple of advantages, and I was able to find ways around the biggest downsides to make the most of the adventure.

Ψ   Ψ   Ψ

I have been on the road a full year when I feel monotony creeping in. The last couple of months have been by far the hardest of the trip. I'm aware that I am not enjoying myself as much as I was for the first six or eight months. Because I have been constantly on the move, always seeing new places and meeting new people, the days are starting to all feel the same.

More importantly, I feel genuine loneliness more often.

I never seriously think about 'giving up', though the thought did occur to me more than once. I have nowhere else to go and nothing else to do with my life, so it feels easier to keep going.

With winter fast approaching in the South, I decide to find a place to stay put for a while. I hope that staying in one place and getting to know the people there will break me out of the 'funk' I have found myself in lately.

As luck would have it, while in *Quito* I learn about The Secret Garden Cotopaxi, a supremely beautiful hostel in the foothills of the massive Cotopaxi volcano. At 19,347ft. Cotopaxi is Ecuador's second highest peak, and is simply stunning. It's also an active volcano and has a glacier perched on top of the perfect cone, making it the most picturesque mountain I have ever seen. A volunteer position has opened at the hostel, so I sign-up immediately.

The hostel is owned and run by a friendly and easy-going Australian / Ecuadorian couple who quickly become good friends. From the second I arrive I know I have found paradise. The hostel is a collection of hand-made adobe buildings pushed back into the hillside, with a stunning view of Cotopaxi front and center. Every day I'm up early - courtesy of our friendly rooster - to watch the most amazing sunrises of my life. Over the course of my days I chat with guests, organize Spanish-speaking staff, work outside on the farm and often go for a two hour hike to jump off our nearby waterfall. That's on the days I don't go hiking, horse-riding or mountain biking on the massive active volcano.

Spending months in the hostel and meeting all kinds of travellers boosts my energy immensely and I dream every night about the adventures that lay ahead. I constantly meet people from so many different walks of life, all having the time of their lives. Some have traveled the world, and some are starting out on their first adventure. All are full of energy and excitement, living every day to the fullest.

If you want to meet a ton of adventurous people and get permanently afflicted with wanderlust, I highly recommend spending time in an International hostel.

My dreams of future adventures grow bigger every day.

Ψ   Ψ   Ψ

I did not intentionally set out to drive from Alaska to Argentina solo, it just turned out that way. There are a few negatives to going it alone, but also some major positives.

Without a doubt, going solo is infinitely better than not going at all.

The Simple Life

Central Ecuador
September 2010

CRUNCHING across the thick frost at 5am, hugging myself for warmth and staring intently at The Southern Cross beside the glowing Cotopaxi volcano, I realize this is one of the most friendly and beautiful places I have ever experienced. Added to this, I am spending time with the happiest people I have ever met anywhere on the planet. To say this place is special would be selling it short. Very, very short.

Ψ   Ψ   Ψ

I have been managing the Secret Garden Hostel for a few months, and have become good friends with Sebastian, a local from the nearby town. Needless to say I jump at the chance when he invites me on his annual family camping trip in the foothills behind Cotopaxi. At first we think I will ride in his

Land Cruiser, though when I suggest bringing the Jeep he can't hide his enthusiasm. Ecuadorians openly love my little Jeep, and are constantly asking for rides or negotiating to buy it - for considerably more than it cost. Soon everyone and everything is loaded into the vehicles, including more kids than I can count. For the first leg of our journey we venture into the National Park surrounding the mighty volcano.

Gazing at Cotopaxi volcano day and night for three months has not prepared me for how massive it really is up close. For an hour we drive across, around and in-between enormous dry lava flows and house-sized volcanic red boulders, making me feel like the little Martian rover navigating alien rocks on a ridiculous scale.

When we stop for a leg stretch I'm told we're having fresh trout for dinner. So fresh are these trout, in fact, they are still happily swimming in the river. Furthermore, I have been nominated as part of the fishing crew. The shadows are beginning to lengthen, making me wonder if there is enough daylight to catch all the fish we will need.

"I have a better system for fishing," Sebastian declares after waiting about three minutes with no bites.

My suspicions of delinquency are confirmed when car jumper leads materialize and Sebastian fails to conceal his boyish grin. I'm hesitant to play with electricity and water, though everyone seems fine with it, so I go with the flow.

An enormous amount of steel wool is wrapped around the ends of two sticks before bare wires are twisted around each ball of steel wool. The wires are connected to an inverter on the battery of Sebastian's running Land Cruiser - a setup that electrifies the two 'wands' with 110V of AC. With the inverter able to generate 2000 Watts, it's the same as a regular outlet in a building, in the form of two lethal wands.

I try to stand out of the way, though I'm pushed to the front and unanimously voted 'bag man'. My job is to stand in the knee-deep river, just down-stream of Sebastian who has the wands in the water, eagerly hunting fish in the reeds. As I wade into the water I'm not entirely sure what's going to happen. I studied physics for many years, though somehow we never got to the part where we stand in a river and put electricity directly into it. Just as the power is turned on, I briefly wonder if the new person is always given this job...

Instantly, small trout float to the surface, apparently stunned. For a second, I'm equally stunned.
I can not believe this works!
Soon I'm inundated by floating fish, washing down to me in the fast-flowing river.

Wow!
This *really* works!

The slippery fish float quickly downstream and prove hard to catch. Obviously unhappy with my poor performance, the ladies on shore scream "Dan!, Dan!" every time I miss one. While scrambling back and forth to catch fish, I can't help noticing the women are standing on shore, safely away from the electrical wires and water.

Obviously I ask too many questions about how strong the current is, so Sebastian happily demonstrates by bringing the wands within two feet of my submerged hands. When I snatch my hands out of the water everyone bursts out laughing once again, and I can't help a good chuckle myself. The shock has a strong kick to it - enough for me to reflexively jerk my hands out of the water. It's not *painful*, exactly, though it's not particularly pleasant either.
It makes me happy to confirm rubber gumboots make excellent electrical insulators - I don't feel a thing through my feet no matter how close I get.

For unknown reasons, the whole enterprise is conducted as fast as we can run upstream catching fish, run back to move the truck, yell back and forward about something, and repeat. At first I think it's just more fun this way, then I finally figure it out.

Sebastian beams when I mention this is highly illegal in my country - "Here too."

In an hour we have a collection of trout big enough to satisfy the ladies, who deem the whole operation a great success. I still think more practice as bag man is needed - I did let quite a few get away, including some big ones. Maybe I will try again some day.

$$\Psi \quad \Psi \quad \Psi$$

We climb up and away from the river on a quickly deteriorating road that soon disappears, leaving us to guess our way across green highland fields dotted with muddy swamps. We all push our luck in the mud, and inevitably Sebastian's severely overloaded Land Cruiser sinks to the axles, less than a hundred yards from our destination. With much hand waiving and shouting, one of the other trucks is hitched up enthusiastically to rescue the stricken Cruiser. It's clear everyone wants to see a good show. After five minutes of engine revving and wheel spinning, the Cruiser is not free. If anything, it has sunk deeper into the sticky muck.

Earlier while crossing a big mud patch I used too much throttle in low range first, revving the engine and spitting mud furiously. The locals took this as a sign the Jeep really is a tough little contender, so everyone suggests I should pull out Sebastian's Cruiser.

Much to the delight of the small crowd, the Jeep easily hauls out the Cruiser at just over idle in low-range 4x4 and with a minimum of fuss. This earns the Jeep the nickname *El Tractor*, causing me to look up 'pride' in the Spanish dictionary.

Our destination is a farm consisting of scattered buildings hand-made from mud bricks, rough cut logs and straw roofs. Perched in the foothills of *Kilindaña* volcano, the farm has commanding views across the alpine meadow below to the imposing Cotopaxi in the near-distance. Within five minutes of arrival we tuck into lunch of rice, potatoes and chicken, soon followed with fresh trout soup, rice and potatoes.

Ψ   Ψ   Ψ

After lunch I'm lazing in a food coma when I notice Sebastian is once again the center of much excitement and activity. Sebastian somehow does that a lot. He is proudly carrying the oldest shotgun I have ever seen - a double barrel that is long enough to be a rifle - and of course his grin covers his entire face. This can only mean more trouble.

There are only two cartridges for the shotgun - both slugs - and only one barrel actually functions, though once Sebastian learns there are deer in the distance, he does not let these minor details deter him.

Full of buck fever, five of us set out hiking across the alpine meadow in the late afternoon. Hiking on the uneven, soaking wet surface is extremely hard work. We're at 15,000 feet, which I quickly remember when I'm huffing and puffing after only five minutes. None of the others even notice the elevation, so I push on, determined to keep up.

An hour later we arrive at the foothills of small mountains, where Sebastian and the others excitedly point at three deer far away in a deep valley. I can barely see brown spots, though I am assured they are in fact deer. Everyone agrees Sebastian should go alone to prevent spooking them, and so he sets off while we sit and wait anxiously.

For the next hour we barely catch infrequent glimpses of Sebastian or the deer. Twice they are spooked and move away, causing him to crawl on his belly. After waiting an eternity, a single shot rings out. We're all excited, though I can't believe he has hit a deer at such an incredible distance.

We practically run up the side of the small mountain, eager to see what has happened. Sebastian's grin is visible long before anything else, and success is confirmed when he steps aside to show a good sized deer. He has virtually run down the mountain dragging the deer, bursting with excitement and pride. After congratulations and a lot of back slapping, I notice the deer has already been gutted. Sebastian explains how he used the point on the buckle of his belt - apparently good enough.

We struggle with the deer for a few hundred yards before finding a suitable log to string it over. After snapping the log to length we march across the field, proudly hoisting our prize. Hours in the gym now payoff - it's quickly clear I can bear the weight better than the others. They repeatedly spell off on the front while I labor away in the rear. My being a full foot taller also has something to do with it, I'm sure

We're all exhausted as we drag our feet uphill for the last few hundred yards, though we quickly perk up when we sense the excitement at camp. They have been waiting anxiously all afternoon. In less than five minutes the deer is hung, and Sebastian sets to work butchering the carcass. It's obvious he knows what to do, and explains he has watched his Dad butcher animals on countless occasions. Everyone is bursting with joy at the prospect of meat for dinner, and all want to contribute. Even Sebastian's three year old daughter stands directly at the carcass and touches and prods the various chunks that are cut away. It's clear she is learning lessons that will stay with her for life.

$$\Psi \quad \Psi \quad \Psi$$

In the evening I'm amazed to see gender lines drawn quickly and clearly. The ladies huddle inside to cook dinner over an open fire while the men gather outside to drink. Using just an iron pot and wooden spoon the ladies lean right over the fire on the floor of the mud hut. There is no chimney or ventilation of any kind and smoke chokes the room, causing my eyes to burn furiously. In ten seconds tears are streaking down my cheeks, and I choke on the thick smoke and break into a coughing fit. Amazingly, the ladies are laughing and smiling as they stand in a circle and stir the dinner pot. They don't seem to mind at all.

Outside, the men stand around talking, laughing and drinking. We drink beer and *aguadente* - a strong and crude liquor distilled from sugar cane. This follows the world-wide tradition of fermenting anything and everything possible to make the strongest alcohol imaginable. There is much joke-telling, talk of ladies and finally a guitar is produced for some drunken sing-alongs. Everyone appreciates my strumming, and they recognise a Green Day song, though they don't know the words in English. After a few generous cups of the strong stuff, I can't translate into Spanish on the fly.

Long after dark, when the biting cold finally overtakes the festive mood, the men move inside to perch in dark corners. Everyone falls silent as they tuck into a delicious dinner of deer chunks in stew with fried trout, with a side of rice and potatoes.

Soon I find myself fighting to keep my eyes open, and have no idea what time it is when I crawl into my tent before worming deep into my sleeping bag. In spite of the bitter cold I fall asleep in less than ten seconds, utterly wiped out.

Ψ   Ψ   Ψ

The severe cold and unfamiliarity of my tent mean I don't get much sleep. I'm going soft after three months of luxury sleeping in a real bed at the hostel. Everything is coated in a thick layer of ice at 5am, and the view is staggeringly beautiful. I spend the next hour taking photos while furiously rubbing my hands to regain feeling. When I return to the farmhouse, the ladies have breakfast well under control, again leaning directly over the open fire. Nobody seems to notice it's rice, potatoes and trout soup again, because they are too busy talking excitedly, laughing and grinning.

After everyone thoroughly thaws out, the day's activities take shape. We will all hike to find elusive *Chiwilas*, cause for great excitement. I am told they are a tiny, sweet fruit that will take some finding, but are well worth the effort.

We have been hiking across the soggy meadow - kids and all - for twenty minutes when a hilarious game of horse and bull breaks out, based around an old bull horn found on the ground. Kids ride on the shoulders of an adult while someone gives chase pretending to be a bull by holding the horn on their head. Snorting, grunting and laughing are all acceptable bull noises. Everyone scrambles and bursts into laughter whenever the 'bull' spontaneously decides to give chase, though it rarely catches anyone. An hour and a half later the game continues, even after hiking many miles over difficult terrain.

Over the mountains and far, far away we arrive at our destination - a scrubby outcrop of brush and trees, rare at this elevation. In the very center is a huge cluster of cactus into which everyone dives, attacking cacti left, right and centre. I learn the highly sought-after *Chiwilas* are actually the tiny fruit of the cactus. They grow far down in the center of the plant, and are well protected by the many spikes.

With only bare hands and a small stick, I soon have fingers full of spines and no desire for more *Chiwilas*. I'm honestly not that impressed with them anyway. They are extremely small, and after biting through the pulp-like crust yield barely a drop of sweet nectar. I nap under a tree, and can not believe my eyes two hours later when everyone is still energetically diving into the cacti, lugging around sack fulls of the tiny fruit. Of course, they have hundreds of spines in their hands, though it's not mentioned even once.

Even after my nap I'm exhausted on the walk back, though

none of the locals show any sign of fatigue. They happily eat left-over potatoes from coat pockets and drink from the many ditches we cross. Lunch - as you might guess - is rice and potatoes. We have run out of trout.

I'm struck time and time again by how happy and playful these Ecuadorians are. Not just the kids either, even the adults get right in on the fun, playing the bull or running around simply for fun. Sebastian and the guys demonstrate this intense happiness perfectly by collecting and donning moss on their faces for the best Gandalf impersonations in history. Roaring laughter all round shows how much it is appreciated.

Ψ   Ψ   Ψ

Even after cramming into a car for a long and bumpy ride, eating the same plain food for every meal, sleeping in freezing conditions, traipsing for hours through mud and getting hundreds of spines in their fingers, every single person is still beaming. They are extremely happy to be out in nature surrounded by family.

I honestly believe these people who have so little are the happiest people I have ever met.

I have so much to learn.

Climbing Cotopaxi Volcano

Central Ecuador
September 2010
19,347ft. / 5,897m.

T HE wedge being driven deep into my skull is splitting it wide open. I have never experienced pain and exhaustion like this in my entire life, and it's getting worse by the minute. To add to my misery, my climbing partner - connected to me with a ten foot rope - is now drinking hard alcohol. The other team of climbers have fallen far behind, and have most likely given up. I huff and puff simply to drag my ice axe forward. Utterly defeated, I wonder if we should also call an end to this madness.

Ψ Ψ Ψ

For the last four months I have watched with great interest as climbing groups make summit attempts on *Cotopaxi* volcano.

With each departure my fascination has only increased. Each and every time I wait anxiously, eager for the climbers to return. Soon I find myself propped on the edge of my seat, listening as every detail of their ordeal is recounted. Some tales are told with broad grins and high fives, while others are sad stories of fear and defeat told with slumped shoulders. Always, the tales are a mixture of triumph and failure.

More than any other, one quote has been repeated by those who return:

> *"Climbing Cotopaxi is the most difficult thing*
> *I have ever done in my life."*

Since arriving at the Secret Garden Hostel I have stared at the spectacular mountain every single day. From sunrise to sunset, it dominates the skyline, utterly captivating me. From the minute I laid eyes on Cotopaxi I knew I would make an attempt on the summit and in preparation I have been training since day one.

Running at 12,000ft. is exhausting at first, and I struggle to fill my lungs after only two minutes of slow jogging. As the weeks turn into months, I'm able to run further and further, eventually approaching six miles per run. My body is acclimatizing by producing more red blood cells to transport what little oxygen my lungs are able to bring in. For further training, I enter a six mile community fun-run with a friend. The run is in *Quito* - all the way down at 9,350ft. where I set a personal best, running hard for the entire distance.

For more training, I repeatedly hike from the hostel to the summit of nearby *Pasochoa* volcano. The hike is virtually straight up, with 4,500ft. of elevation change in six hours. Once, over an entire day, I hike/jog from the hostel to the refuge on the slopes of Cotopaxi itself at 15,760ft., climbing almost 6,000ft.

I have spent four months living at high elevation and have trained hard for this climb.

I will never be better acclimatized than I am now.

The waiting is over.
Now it is my turn.

$$\Psi \quad \Psi \quad \Psi$$

It's a beautiful sunny morning when our guides arrive sometime after my tenth nervous cup of tea and fifth banana. I have teamed up with three others at the hostel for a summit attempt. We are split into teams of two, with each team assigned a professional guide. I feel confident Canadian winters have prepared me for the biting cold we expect, and I'm not at all surprised by the mountain of gear the guides have brought.

Our guides Franklin and Victor are both around my age, and look extremely fit and strong. They grew up nearby, and high elevation is a way of life for them. Both are softly spoken, and although they speak perfect English, it becomes clear that neither feels the need to speak just to fill silence. I soon learn neither will speak unless directly spoken to, or unless they have something important to say. I like both of them immensely, and feel extremely confident in their abilities to keep us safe on the mountain.

While trying on gear we pepper them with questions before realizing we never should have asked.

"How many times have you been to the summit?"
"More than one hundred each."

"How many people make it?"
"Less than half."

"How long will it take?"
"About five or six hours from the refuge to the summit. More than seven and we must turn back."

"How much sleep will we get tonight?"
"A couple of hours, if you're lucky."

"How cold will it be?"
"About 15°F for the hike, maybe -15°F at the summit."

"What happens if we get altitude sickness?"
"Headache, dizziness, vomiting. We go back."

(and me) "What's for dinner?"

The drive to the now familiar parking lot at 14,760ft. is full of tension and anxiety that only amplifies as we load our packs and trudge up to the *José Rivas* refuge, a thousand feet higher. After a short rest we make our way across to the glacier at 16,400ft. to practice moving on the ice. None of us have used crampons or an ice axe before, so we start from square one. We walk up, down and sideways, feeling unsure about walking on steep, slippery ice. I practice over and over until I'm satisfied with my gear and new found abilities. Well, I practice until Franklin tells me to stop so I don't tire myself out, that is.

The refuge is an enormous building accommodating day-trippers to the glacier and summiters alike. Upstairs, bunk beds are stacked three high, with wafer-thin mattresses and no heating. After a delicious carb-loaded meal of pasta carbonara and a brief look at the stars above *Quito*, we climb into our frigid sleeping bags at 7:30pm. I feel nervous, excited and scared all at once and I hope like mad for a few hours of sleep.

I drift in and out, not quite sure if I'm awake or dreaming. My disorientation is compounded by demented dreams that slip out of reach when I'm awake. I remember enough to know they involve my Dad and family, leaving me feeling uneasy and restless. The extreme elevation is already messing with my head.

$$\Psi \quad \Psi \quad \Psi$$

My eyes are wide open when Franklin sounds the wake-up at midnight. I have been laying awake listening to the intense wind howling against the building and have convinced myself our plans are dashed by the always-hostile weather. I'm certain it will be impossible to climb today. I shrug and go through the motions of gearing up anyway, secretly feeling a little relieved I have a good excuse to go back to bed.

I put on two pairs of wool socks under two-layer mountaineering boots, fleece pants covered by waterproof pants, a thermal long-sleeve shirt, regular long-sleeve woolen shirt and fleece top all covered by a waterproof jacket, two pairs of gloves, a face mask and helmet with my headlamp attached. On the way out I grab my backpack with food, water and extra warm clothes. With my ice axe, crampons and climbing harness, I will be ready to go.

A trip to the bathroom reveals a perfectly clear, starry night. The light breeze sounded a hundred times worse than it actually is, and we have ideal climbing conditions. I wash my face in a bucket of icy water, waking me up and taking away all feeling in my hands for the next twenty minutes.

We're excited over breakfast, though our guides remain non-committal about the weather.
"Things change fast on the mountain."
"Anything can happen up here."
After a final bathroom break we step into our climbing harnesses and leave the safety of the refuge just after 1am.

It's faster and easier to climb up the slippery scree stones than to walk on the glacier itself, so we stay off it as long as possible. The first hour is a slow, single-file trudge up a gravel slope without using crampons. The night is clear and moonless and everything outside the small circle of light cast by my headlamp is utterly black. I stumble badly while trying to hike, take in the view of *Quito* and stargaze all at the same time.

I realize it's time to get my head in the game.
This is really it.

Before stepping onto the glacier we sit down for a short rest and to attach crampons to our boots. We're all feeling comfortable after our practice session only yesterday until the guides bring over rope and tie us together. The rope drives home the seriousness and danger of what we are doing. We are split into two teams - each with a guide in front and two climbers behind.

The first section of glacier is so steep we can't walk straight up as we normally would. We face side-on to the mountain and walk sideways, constantly crossing and un-crossing one foot in front of the other, while using our ice-axes as walking sticks for balance. Soon it's obvious my team is faster, so we overtake on a switchback turn. Quickly the headlamps of the other team fade, leaving us alone with the cold wind whipping across our faces.

The steep trail eventually gives way to switchbacks, which provide a tiny relief at every turn. I have to swap the ice axe from one hand to the other and walk 'sideways' the other way each time we double-back. I distract myself concentrating on this for what seems like hours, focusing on my footing and using the ice axe in the correct hand - always the uphill side.

We encounter small crevasses where Franklin plays out thirty feet of rope while we take a giant step across. After pausing to look down, the concept of a bottomless crevasse keeps my mind busy for half an hour. I struggle to understand that I really could not see the bottom and I step a little wider and a little more carefully over the next one.

Still moving relatively well, we enter a region with towering ice formations and like a switch being turned off, the wind instantly stops. Franklin allows a short break, a concept that had not occurred to me. While eating a chocolate bar and sipping water Franklin says we're at approximately 17,700ft. and are making good time. It takes me almost two minutes to calculate we're more than halfway to the summit, boosting my spirits immensely.
This is not so hard after all, I naively muse.

For almost an hour we traipse through the strange ice formations where I catch only glimpses of the towering ice. My headlamp simply does not penetrate far enough into the pitch black night. Eventually, my skill with crampons and ice axe reaches a point where I don't need to actively concentrate. For the first time, I have spare brain power to think about whatever I want.

Immediately, before I'm aware my brain has started thinking again, one thought pops up that will not go away.
Why on Earth am I doing this?

I have never before wondered why I want to climb an enormous, glacier covered active volcano in the middle of the night. Until now 'becuase it's there' has been good enough. As it turns out, I have no better reason. This is pure madness. I can't think of a better explanation. This thought, and the slight pounding in my head do not help my motivation.

During the next hour, the going gets tough. Seriously tough. With each step, the air I'm sucking into my lungs gets thinner and thinner. The route gets more technical, and the physical exhaustion creeps up on me. It's obvious - at least in my mind - that my partner Mike is really struggling. I begin to worry how this will impact my climb. If he turns back, my summit attempt will be finished. We must stick together.

After finishing a narrow, exposed and nasty sloping section we both crumple onto the ice for the first time.
"This is too hard." Mike gasps while desperately trying to suck air into his lungs.
"You don't say!" I shoot back - the reply loaded with emotion and anger. This automatic response reflects my ragged state of mind, and I'm too exhausted to take it back.

I only met Mike at the hostel a few days ago, and lacking any options, I decided we would be partners. Mike is a bit older and slower than me, though he certainly makes up in mental strength. Mike has a solid air of determination I admire, though also some habits I do not. I stare in disbelief as he takes a flask from his pack and takes a swig.

"Want some whiskey?" he asks.
No. I do not want some whiskey.

I'm furious he is drinking, and Mike just replies smugly that climbers have been doing it for decades so it must work, before he takes another shot. I can only hope he does not ruin my chance of reaching the summit. There is literally nothing I can do about it now, so I let it drop.

Franklin can see the exhaustion painted on our faces, and allows a long rest so we can assess our situation. He says we are still moving well, and it's about an hour and twenty minutes to the summit. The sun will soon make an appearance, though we will not feel any warmth until much later.

After a break of only ten minutes my feet and hands are completely numb and even Franklin is beating his chest to fight off the cold. We slowly move along and soon the trail is ridiculously steep and tough. This section is terribly exposed to the elements, and we creep up an incline so steep that even the 'shuffle sideways' technique is a struggle. I'm moving so slowly it's painful, so I resort to my old hiking habit of counting my steps. This keeps my brain occupied and distracts me from my now splitting headache.

Our progress slows to a comical pace. For over an hour, my life consists of only the following four steps:

1. Move ice axe forward one foot and lean heavily on it, breathing hard (count one).
2. Move right foot up slope, crossing in front of left foot, breathing hard (count two).
3. Move left foot up slope behind right foot, breathing hard (count three).
4. Rest on ice axe for a three count, trying to suck in oxygen before repeating.

While struggling forward in this fashion, the sun begins to brighten the sky, doing wonders for our morale. Although Franklin does not say, and there are many false summits, we know we're closing in on our goal. We continue the painfully slow shuffle forward and upward. Soon the horizon is glowing blood-red and we see the view below for the first time - simply breathtaking. As the sun climbs higher we see the enormous triangle shadow cast by the mountain and even find the energy for a joke.

"The sun rises at 9:30am when you live behind Cotopaxi."

Further boosting morale, we glimpse three headlamps bobbing through the gloom below - our companions have not given up and are still climbing!

Counting my steps helps immensely and breaks the difficulty down into manageable pieces. Finally as we near the summit the mountain levels out and I'm soon counting to ten before resting, then twenty. My brain has as much trouble as my body when I count one hundred steps without a rest - I collapse on the spot struggling for air, unable to comprehend one hundred and one.

After a short break we march on, and in less than two minutes I'm standing next to an enormous crater, with nowhere higher to step. I watch dazed as Franklin un-clips my carabiner before crumpling to my knees. I'm overcome with exhaustion and emotion. I feel a mixture of elation, exhaustion, relieft and fear for the trek down. For thirty seconds I gape open-mouthed, not thinking much of anything.

When we finally snap out of our trance we embrace and tramp around taking photos and pointing at distant landmarks we recognise. The day is so clear we can easily see every major volcano in Ecuador, including those hundreds of miles distant. I'm especially excited to see Chimborazo volcano, the highest mountain in Ecuador at 20,564ft., a sight I have literally dreamed for months.

We have reached the summit in five hours and fifteen minutes, a little faster than average, Franklin says. It's extremely cold due to the strong wind and elevation, causing Mike to soon walk fifty yards down to find what little reprieve he can. I'm determined to stay longer and talk with Franklin, naming every mountain and city we can see. Upon closer inspection, I even see a wisp of smoke leaving Cotopaxi's crater. The full realization I have summited the world's highest active volcano fills me with happiness and leaves me buzzing.

Too soon the cold becomes unbearable and we begin the arduous hike down the same route we just came up. Franklin ties himself at the end of the rope so he can arrest our trio if we fall and slide uncontrollably. He judges I am in better condition than Mike, so I'm in the all-important lead position.

I take stock of my physical condition. I am exhausted. My legs are jelly and my head is splitting open with a headache that threatens to floor me. Not ideal for hiking down a steep, icy slope. I remember most mountaineering accidents happen on the way down when everyone has pushed beyond their limit. Concentrating on every step, I never put a single foot wrong.

Soon after leaving the summit we pass our companions and offer words of encouragement. The utter exhaustion on their faces acts like a mirror for ours. The sun has risen and we can now see the amazing ice formations that surround us. We stop often to take photos, secretly thrilled for the rest breaks. While lazing in the sun taking a long rest, our friends amble around the corner, broad grins visible from a long way off. We are jubilant at our shared success, while cautious of the descent below.

We soak in the view and re-charge in the early morning sunshine, thoroughly enjoying the chocolate we gorge on. Even in the bright sunlight, I still can't see the bottom of the crevasses we hop across.

My headache continues to build until I'm struggling to function properly. I can't focus my eyes, and I can't stop feeling furious about a million inconsequential things. With each step I feel my brain jolt into my skull, increasing the pain as I continue down.

At the edge of the glacier we again sit for a long rest, full of smiles and awe at our achievement. Now without crampons, the final descent is hiking directly down the slippery gravel, commonly called scree-running. I'm so exhausted and my legs are so fatigued I slip and fall ten times in five minutes, throwing an even darker cloud over my mood. Nobody else is struggling like me, and they soon power ahead.

I'm swept up in my thoughts on the way down, wondering why I set out to do something so pointless and difficult. I feel certain about a few things. Climbing to the summit of Cotopaxi is by far the most difficult thing I have ever done in my life. The view from the top was possibly the most beautiful I have ever seen in my life. Without a doubt, climbing Cotopaxi is the single most rewarding thing I have ever done.

I am certain there is a connection. I believe the most difficult things are often the most rewarding.

By the time I arrive at the refuge half an hour later my headache is so bad it completely overpowers my bad mood. I force a smile and laugh with the group already lazing about in the morning sunshine.

A few day-trippers mill around, openly staring at us.
"Yes," I can finally say, grinning broadly.
"We summited Cotopaxi volcano today."

On Happiness

F ROM time to time on my travels I meet people I feel drawn
to. These are people who appear to have more fun than
everyone else put together and who have the ability to change
the happiness of others for the better.

Dimly, I've always been aware that sometimes I enjoy myself
immensely while in the company of these people, while with
other people I'm left feeling empty and inadequate. At these
times I feel less happy even though that person seems to
be having a great time. After years of these experiences, I
can't pinpoint a reason for the difference and I have spent
years wondering, always thinking there must be a secret about
happiness I don't know. I desperately want to understand.
Luckily, my brother Mike learned an important lesson about
happiness and was only too eager to teach me his perspective.

"When interacting with others, there are two contrasting ways a person can make themselves happy," he begins.

"I call the first kind *Subtractive Happiness*."

"These people make themselves happier by stealing happiness from others. Under the guise of jokester or leader, they put people down, criticize and make 'clever', snide and sarcastic remarks. They want to always be the center of attention, and will stop anyone else taking center stage."

"They belittle and ridicule others while big-noting themselves. Often they laugh at people rather than with them, and they actively encourage others to do the same."

"These people are bullies. They are so subtle about it that most of us are not consciously aware it's happening."

"Once they have torn other people down and built themselves up, they feel better," Mike explains.

"In short, they steal or subtract happiness from others to increase their own."

"The second way a person can make themselves happy around others is the exact opposite, and I call it *Additive Happiness*."

"These people continually work to make those around them happier. They are quick to give praise, offer encouragement and are sincere with their admiration. This kind of person loves to share the spotlight, and actively encourages others to talk about themselves, their achievements and their aspirations, no matter how small."

"These people lift the happiness of an entire room, making themselves happier in the process."

"In short, they give or add happiness to other people to increase their own."

This explanation fit my experiences perfectly. At Kirkwood I had a blast snowboarding, even though I was terrible at it. I have often wondered why I did not hate failing so badly, and actually enjoyed trying. With Mike's perspective I now realize it's because the people I snowboarded with offered so much encouragement and praise for my attempts. They made me feel so good about myself I could not help but be happy.

The crew at Kirkwood were the genuine article, and are the kind of people I have always felt drawn to.

Ψ   Ψ   Ψ

Next time you meet someone that appears happier than average, think about what kind of person you are spending time with.

Are they greedily stealing your happiness, or are they actively making those around them happier?

Familiar Games

B EING constantly on the move means I'm constantly saying
goodbye. There is no getting around it, and it sucks.
Leaving The Secret Garden Cotopaxi is no exception. I have
made great friends over the last four months who I'm really
going to miss. Five minutes before leaving I mention it's a
shame I won't see the improvements we have been working on
get finished. Off-hand the boss says,
"You'll be back one day."
My reply comes naturally, before I even think about it
"Yeah, I will."
I sing songs to myself while driving away in an attempt to
force a smile onto my face.

I move South to the familiar town of *Baños*, where I spend
a couple of nights at *La Casa Verde*, an extremely peaceful

eco-hostel run by an Aussie and Kiwi couple. Spending time alone reading and writing helps move my head back into 'road mode', where I need it to be. Further South I find the Incan ruins at *Ingapirca*, a site Ecuadorians are extremely proud of. I spend a wonderful lazy afternoon wandering around in the sunshine and striking up conversations with locals.

Soon I'm warned of a planned protest tomorrow which will barricade the main highway. The local indigenous people are again unhappy with the government and will blockade all roads in and out of the area for seventy-two hours, starting at midnight tonight. I'm told they will make no exceptions for foreigners and my tires will be slashed if I attempt to push through. The locals are firm on this and insist it's a serious matter. I make camp right in the parking lot of the ruins, which turns out to be the perfect place - extremely quiet overnight.

In the morning I'm almost disappointed to see no road closures whatsoever after such a big build up, though of course I'm relieved to have no trouble.

Late in the afternoon I arrive in the sleepy village of *Vilcabamba*, famous for 'trapping' visitors with it's beautiful scenery and friendly atmosphere. After chatting to locals in the town square I learn of The Rumi-Wilco Eco-Reserve, an extremely beautiful place to camp and exolore.

The following morning I hike high into the cloud forest surrounding town to the edge of the remotest of all National Parks, *Podocarpus*. Every statistic about this National Park is mind-blowing. There are more species of orchids in the park than the rest of the world put together, for example. Hard to believe, but true nonetheless.

To avoid getting trapped I leave early the following morning making one last stop at the book exchange. The quick stop turns into an hour long conversation with the owner, an extremely friendly and talkative American ex-pat. He tries hard to convince me to stay, and I practically run to escape causing the other locals in the store to burst out laughing and ask how soon I will be back.

Ψ   Ψ   Ψ

I wind South through mountains and picturesque small villages, in no particular hurry. With twilight fast approaching I struggle to find an adequate place to camp, always a cause for concern. The dirt road cut into the side of the mountains simply does not have any side roads where I can get out of view. I'm close to the border, and I worry sketchy people may be in the area.

I find a small pull-out near a beautiful river, though it's a little too close to the road and visible, so I decide to move on. Ten minutes later when no better option presents itself, I turn back - it will simply have to do. Just as I finish setting up my tent an old man startles me by calling out a greeting and asking what I'm doing. I ask his permission to camp, though he explains he is only working the land, he does not own it. At the same time he assures me it's no problem to camp here. Although I occasionally see and hear traffic on the nearby road, I sleep soundly, without visitors during the night.

Ψ   Ψ   Ψ

In the early morning I wind along an isolated dirt track with zero other vehicles. Eventually I arrive at a tiny Military checkpoint in the middle of nowhere. It's nothing more than a log across the road in front of a shack made of sticks. The friendly officers check my paperwork and point me towards a knife-edge ridge line surrounded by thickly forested mountains.

I reach the small and isolated town of *La Balsa* (The Ferry), consisting of a handful of buildings perched on the edge of the river serving as the border with Peru. In recent years a bridge had been built, though the town retains it's original name. The bridge is blocked by another 'boom gate' made from a large tree trunk. I'm soon told the Immigration officers are having breakfast, so I must wait half an hour.

I strike up a conversation with a lady running a small shack I take to be the general store for town. We chat casually about many varied topics and I realize after months managing Ecuadorian staff in the hostel my Spanish has again improved leaps and bounds. I can now talk about almost anything I want. When I don't know a particular word locals are perfectly happy to help as I stumble around it. They also don't seem to mind my imperfect pronunciation in the least.

When breakfast is finished I hand over the Jeep paperwork to *Aduana* (Customs) and recieve an exit stamp in my passport in about three minutes flat. The Immigration officer carefully inspects my Visa and stamps - I'm told there is a $200 USD fine for overstaying. At first he is visibly excited when he sees my original visa has expired, thinking he will make big money today. When I point out my extension complete with fancy hologram sticker he is a little disappointed, though accepts it nonetheless.

Walking back to the Jeep I flip through my passport which I have not looked in for months. I'm amazed to see I have been in Ecuador for a touch over five months.
Wow, that five months really flew by.

I cross the bridge and park in front of another log boom gate on the Peruvian side. I'm the only 'guest' for miles and so I am immediately helped by everyone. I complete a tourist card at Immigration, walk down the hill for a Police stamp and then wander back to Immigration for a passport stamp. Next door at Customs I hand over a copy of my license, passport and registration and the slightly deaf officer on duty has me fill out my own paperwork with all the mundane details of the Jeep (color, year, make, VIN number, etc.). Half an hour later we stick a giant Customs sticker on the windshield before I drive under the gate, officially in Peru.

An extremely easy and friendly border crossing, and free across the board.

Driving away I see a lone backpacker waiting patiently in the shade. Fabricio is a friendly French traveler who made the trip to this remote border to extend his stay in Peru. He left Peru and waited in Ecuador for an hour, then came right back and got stamped back into Peru for another ninety days - a common travellers' trick. It's always nice to have a fellow wanderer ride along and his stories of adventures in Peru keep us chatting in Spanish for hours.

Ψ   Ψ   Ψ

The tiny dirt road slowly deteriorates, turning from extremely potholed gravel into flat and slick clay and mud created by recent rain. In 4x4 the Jeep moves along without a problem, though I can feel it sliding on the slick surface. At one particularly steep hill all the vehicles without 4x4 are stuck at the bottom or waiting at the top, too afraid to attempt the descent. To make things interesting, a large truck is stuck about half way up, right in the middle of the narrow road. Apparently he was trying to go up and started sliding sideways. Fearful of sliding into the ditch the driver immediately stopped and the wheels are now chocked with large rocks. It's clear the truck will not be moving anytime soon.

The road only goes back to Ecuador and there is no other way around. I'm not good at waiting, and I am confident in the Jeep. I have no trouble with grip in 4x4, though the truck blocking the road presents a problem. When I try to sneak around the side the two rear wheels slide into the sloping ditch. The locals are delighted to watch as I slide sideways up the hill with my front wheels on the road and rear wheels in the sloping ditch. All four wheels furiously spit mud, completely caking the Jeep from front to back.

Over the crest I descend an equally slippery slope down the

other side. I'm strongly reminded of packed snow and ice in Canada, and I take it carefully. It's obvious the locals have not had much practice with snow driving, evidenced by the many abandoned vehicles that have slid into the ditches.

Passing through villages and towns in this mountainous region of Peru I'm strongly reminded of countless towns in Southern Mexico or Panama. The landscape is tropical - with bananas, pineapples and rice growing in the fields surrounding the road. Towns bustle with cars, trucks and tuk-tuks zipping every which way.

Ψ   Ψ   Ψ

I bid farewell to Fabricio at a bus terminal before continuing on a new highway winding through a spectacular river canyon. Concentrating on the scenery and driving, I'm surprised to round a bend and see Policemen wave me down. The three officers do nothing to contain their excitement, making it abundantly clear how they feel - they think they're on a winner. Nobody mentioned insurance for the Jeep at the border, and I completely forgot to ask if it was mandatory. After five months in Ecuador, I'm rusty on border crossings.

The Policemen are onto it immediately, so I hand over my Ecuadorian insurance, hoping they won't notice. They have clearly seen this before, and will not accept that attempt. Quick as a flash, one of them whips out a Peruvian law book and conveniently even has the passage highlighted and underlined. I can read it easily in Spanish:

> *"Tourists driving in Peru must have insurance.*
> *If you do not, the penalty follows..."*

I am happily chatting away in Spanish, forgetting my usual routine of pretending to not understand. Again, I realize, I'm rusty at this game after so long relaxing in Ecuador. Now they know I understand Spanish, they have no trouble explaining I must pay a fine, and it's going to be big. I have no idea how to deal with this, so I just let the conversation develop naturally, hoping I can figure something out.

At first we're standing around the Jeep, and the officers look at it greedily. After only a short time, they ask me to give them things to pay the fine. One asks for the spare tire, while another wants my tent and headlamp. There is no way I'm giving those away, so the negotiations continue for a long time. I'm in no particular hurry, though I sense the officers getting anxious about extracting their money from me soon. I gather most people simply pay up quickly so they can move along, and I feel that wasting their time will work to my advantage.

Eventually we walk to their patrol car, a beat up old sedan. Here they tell me they don't even have money for gas, or lunch. They want me to give or buy them both, and ask repeatedly. Again, there is little chance of that happening.

One of the officers produces an 'Infraction' book and makes a big show about writing a ticket, pen poised over the paper while the other two try to convince me I really don't want that. A ticket is a dreadful thing, they say, and it would be best if he did not actually write one.

"It's OK," I say.
"I will take the ticket to the next town and pay at the bank."
"Then I will buy insurance and everything will be OK. I made a mistake. I'm sorry."

"Oh, no!" the three sing in chorus.
"You must pay it here!"

Having anticipated this reaction, I have my reply ready.
I explain politely I don't carry any cash with me. I only carry Credit Cards as protection against being robbed. This way I am much safer, I explain.

All three are visibly shocked at this development, and do not hide their frustration at all.
"You have no cash?!" they all exclaim before bursting out

laughing.

After wishing me a safe journey, the officers hand back my paperwork, dive into their car and speed off in a cloud of dust.

New country, same games.

Jeep lashed into a container, set for Panama to Colombia

Waiting at an International border

Sunset over Cotopaxi volcano seen from the Hostel

Ecuadorian family during our camping trip

On the summit of Cotopaxi Volcano, 19,347ft.

At Suila Grande - Joe Simpson's *Touching The Void*

At Peru's tallest mountain - Huascaran, 22,205ft.

The Jeep on the Salt Flats of Uyuni, Bolivia

On the Salt Flats with my companions

Torres Del Paine, Patagonia

The immense Southern Patagonian Icefield

End of the Pan-American Highway, Tierra del Fuego, Argentina

With the completed map on the hood of the Jeep

The Cordillera Huayhuash

The Peruvian Andes
October 2010

D EEP in the mountains of central Peru lies the *Cordillera Huayhuash* (Huayhuash Mountain Range, pronounced 'why-wash'). This extremely rugged and remote range includes the infamous *Siula Grande* mountain (20,814ft.), made famous in the most harrowing mountain climbing tale ever told - Joe Simpson's *Touching The Void*[8]. After Joe broke his leg horribly just below the summit, his climbing partner was left with no choice and cut their climbing rope, leaving Joe to plummet thousands of feet to certain death.

The story and it's aftermath are still extremely controversial to this day. Many people believe Joe's partner was wrong to cut the rope, while many others insist it was the only course

---

[8] *Touching The Void: The True Story of One Man's Miraculous Survival* Joe Simpson, 1989

of action, and therefore the right course of action. The entire mountain range is extremely isolated and pummeled by storms, a fitting location for such a harrowing tale.

It's possible to hike around the massive range on foot and the *Huayhuash* hiking circuit rates second in the world, behind only The Annapurna Loop in Nepal.

The hiking circuit boasts intimidating stats:

- Total distance of 88 miles.
- Total elevation change of over 33,000 feet.
- Hiking always between 13,000 and 16,500 feet.
- Nine major mountain passes.
- All in ten days.

The mountain range lies in a remote and difficult-to-visit region of Peru, with only a single access point. Once I begin, I must finish this hike under my own steam, one way or another.

The hike is commonly organized for a group of about ten people who hire a guide, cook, donkey train and enough gear and food to supply a small army. Hikers carry a small day pack while the remainder of their gear is carted by the donkeys. All meals are cooked and even tents are setup and taken down by the guide. The hikers need only to put one foot in front of the other - literally everything else is taken care of.

As you can imagine, this is not my style of hiking, not even close. I have zero interest in completing the circuit this way.

For me, the only way is with everything on my own back, solo. This will be the most challenging hike of my life, by a very long margin.

Ψ   Ψ   Ψ

After gearing up with supplies and info in *Huaraz*, I wind along bumpy mountainous roads to the tiny town of *Llamac*, the only access to the trail serving as both the start and end point of my hike. After chatting with the friendly owner of the only store in town, I park the Jeep in his secure lot - actually his house compound.

He insists I camp on the town soccer field nearby where I spend the afternoon and evening organizing and re-organizing my gear. Ten days will be the longest self-supported hike I have attempted, so I meticiously measure food for each day. Combined with all my camping gear, I struggle to fit everything into my old hiking pack. Food is by far my most important consideration when hiking - I eat huge quantities, and I need to pack in as many calories as possible. Luckily there are plenty of mountain streams and lakes I can drink from, so I will not have to carry much drinking water. Chlorine tablets to treat the water should make it safe enough. I hope my pack will not burst at the seams - or even worse - be too heavy to carry.

I can barely sleep, unable to contain my excitement for the massive task ahead.

Day 1 - 3,300ft. up / 825ft. down / 6.5 hrs

I rise with the sun, and wave goodbye to the Jeep in the secure lot at 8:30am. To fit everything in my backpack, I have both my tent and sleeping pad strapped to the outside, something I never normally do. I don't like them being exposed to the elements, and it makes the whole thing feel unbalanced. Even on flat ground, the brutally heavy pack feels unwieldy, and threatens to topple me whenever I get a little off balance.

I obsessively adjust the straps, hoping to make the weight more comfortable, until I resign myself to the fact it's just heavy. I walk through the middle of town, feeling conspicuous with all this junk on my back. I must look stupid struggling with such a huge pack. Happily, my excitement and wonder far outweigh my self-consciousness.

I'm deflated only thirty minutes later when I have to back-track because I took a wrong turn. I'm aware this is no time to be hiking further than nessescarry. Soon I find the correct path, which immediately climbs steeply up a rocky canyon. The lush green valley of town quickly fades and I find myself in a sweltering, dry canyon. The trail braids endlessly and I have no idea which is correct. Not wanting to waste time thinking about it and being indecisive, I just keep climbing and forging ahead. Surely any trail that goes up is the right trail.

The trail is seriously steep, and the top of the ridge does not seem to get any closer as the day wears on. My fresh legs allow me to push hard, and I'm soon pouring sweat. The canyon is dry and dusty, and the only vegetation is scrubby brush and many spiky cacti.

When I finally top out on *Pampa Llamac Pass* I get my first view of the enormous mountain range stretching far into the distance. I'm blown-away to see the gigantic mountains of sheer rock covered in snow and ice jutting into the clouds. I have hiked up 3,300 vertical feet, almost straight up to 13,375 feet.
I will not drop below this elevation for the next ten days.

After a relaxing forty-five minutes of almost level hiking, I make camp at a beautiful aqua lake, *Laguna Yahuacocha*. A few other hikers are camping, and a local family lives in a hut just back from the edge of the lake. After ditching my pack and setting up my tent, I stroll in the fading light taking photos and chatting to hikers about the trail. They fill my head with tales of what lies ahead, and are all dumbfounded to learn I'm hiking alone, without a guide or donkey train.

The sun sets and the temperature drops rapidly - soon I'm wearing my best thermals for sleeping. Even still, I'm forced to rush dinner so I can dive into my sleeping bag sooner.

I have a drawn-out and cold night caused by a hole in my sleeping pad. I must have torn it scraping against the spiky cacti in the canyon. I have a patch kit, though of course I left it in the Jeep. In the middle of the night I consider going back for it, though eventually decide I will simply have to blow it up five times each night for the rest of the hike.

Day 2 - 2,300ft. up / 1,800ft. down / 7 hrs

I rise before the sun and discover a thick layer of ice covering my tent at 6am. During the night I pulled all the strings on my sleeping bag closed until I was breathing through a tiny hole - a sure sign of the biting cold. I wander the campsite and lake taking photos in the early morning light, all the while jogging and beating my chest to warm up.

Sunrise is spectacular, but does not bring any warmth at first. After a quick breakfast of hot oats while drying my tent, I stuff everything away and move along the lake edge by 7am.

Reaching the far end of the lake in good time, I immediately begin the climb up a steep and rocky trail. Soon I'm sweating and puffing hard, even after stripping down to shorts and a t-shirt. Struggling for oxygen is something I will just have to get used to during this hike. While resting I'm entertained watching a shepherd move his flock down into the lush valley. The small, elderly man sports a patch of grey hair and a wispy beard, giving him a wise and seasoned look. He is wearing little more than a blanket, and I wonder how he can tolerate the cold while moving so slowly. From what I can see, he does not mind in the least.

The majority of his flock are content to follow and stay with the group, giving no trouble at all. A couple of the big rams, however, are having none of it, and repeatedly charge the shepherd, trying to headbutt him. Obviously accustomed to this dance, the shepherd is always ready with a huge boulder. When the ram charges, he hurls the rock at the animal's lowered head. The crack as the rock hits the ram full in the head is shockingly loud and I wonder about permanent damage. The rams don't seem to mind at all, and come back for more punishment time and again. The shepherd smiles warmly and waves as he ambles past and I have the distinct impression he does this all day, every day.

The climb is steep and slow going, and soon my legs and back ache painfully. I am forced to stop and rest often, something I'm not at all used to. I move past the beautiful *Laguna Solteracocha*, a glacier lake the striking aqua-blue color that only glacier lakes can be. After another steep climb of over 2,000 feet I finally reach *Punta Rondoy* at 15,675ft. the high point of the day. Here I can only rest long enough for one photo before the bitter wind forces me to keep moving. Pushing hard uphill has drained my energy, and I can barely shuffle my feet as I stumble down into the new valley.

After lunch the long march along the valley bottom drags on and on, eventually bringing me to an unfamiliar dirt road. I have a minor melt-down when the mile markers on the road don't match my map. I slump to the ground and wonder if I'm walking in the wrong direction, but can not bring myself to hike backwards even one step. I decide to keep moving forward and take what comes.

Ten minutes later I'm elated to arrive at a rocky outcropping near a small creek. Imposing snow-covered mountains tower overhead in stark contrast to the lush green paradise in front of me. I have reached *Matacancha Campsite*, my goal and home for the night.

It's only 2pm, though I'm utterly drained of energy. I can do little more than lean against a rock and savor chocolate snacks for the afternoon. The temperature again drops rapidly when the deep shadows envelop the lush valley, and I scramble to put on warm layers and setup my tent.

At sunset, just as I finish dinner, a group of ten Israelis arrive. They have a porter, guide, many donkeys and a mountain of gear. The racket is immense, and I'm a little sad to learn this circus will be shadowing me for the rest of the hike. Again I go to bed early, happy for the warmth of my sleeping bag.

Day 3 - 1,880ft. up / 3,150ft. down / 9 hrs

Well rested after more than ten hours of sleep, I again rise before the sun. It was not so cold overnight and there is less ice on my tent this morning. After another quick breakfast and pack up, I'm on the trail at 6.50am, happy to be in front of the large group. Directly from camp, the trail climbs straight up into the mountains towering above.

At this elevation I simply can't get air into my lungs fast enough, so I force myself to slow down until I find a pace I can maintain. The climb to the pass is extremely steep, and I remember my old trick of counting breaths. By counting each time I breathe out, I'm able to keep my pace constant, and stop myself going so fast I get winded and am forced to stop. I hike until the count of one hundred, then rest for ten breaths before continuing. This sets a pace I can maintain, while allowing time to take in the scenery. It also distracts me just enough to make everything easier.

Just over two hours after leaving camp, and with the summit in sight, the Israelis catch and overtake me. I'm proud to have all my gear on my own back, though it's still demoralizing to be overtaken so easily. I feel like I'm going backwards as they easily power ahead.

Twenty minutes later at the summit (15,460ft.), I realize my backpack feels much better - it's already lighter from the food I have eaten, and I packed it better this morning with heavy items down low and close to my back. Now I don't feel like it's constantly trying to pull me over backwards.

On top of the pass I eat chocolate while sheltering from the wind and I study the terrain in front of me. From prior research I know there is a natural hot spring on the side of a mountain nearby. Always tempted by hot springs I contemplate exploring the area, but realize this is not the time for a wild goose chase. It could easily take the rest of the day hiking in circles to locate the spring.

I can clearly see the trail I'm supposed to take winding below, and I also spot another trail branching off. After carefully studying the map, I decide to take a short-cut in the hope of saving a couple of hours. I dimly wonder why this smaller track is not the main trail, but push the thought out of my head.

My shortcut works brilliantly, and I don't get lost on my way to *Laguna Mitacocha*, my goal for the day. I'm not sure if that's a good thing or not when I see it's only 11.30am. After thinking for a while I realize why the short-cut is much smaller - most groups don't even come here, they go directly to the next major campsite. I'm unsure what to do, and so I ponder my options while eating Mr. Noodle for lunch. I'm worried about how quickly my container of stove fuel is being used up, so I decide not to cook lunch, and simply eat it raw from now on.

Part of me wants to relax in the warm sun, while another part is already bored. I know for sure I will be out of my mind in three more hours. To save weight I didn't bring a book to read, so I have no way to entertain myself besides hiking.

Ah, why not!
I choose to push on to the next campsite. Soon after leaving the lake I join with the main trail before pushing up and over a second pass for the day (*Carhuac*, 15,345ft.), in four more hours. I have pushed hard to this point, and now I'm wiped out, dragging my feet pitifully. I'm moving so slowly even the donkey train overtakes me before I arrive at *Laguna Carhuacocha* after a nine hour day. The last thirty minutes provide spectacular views along the valley I will hike in the morning. The enormous mountains close in as I rapidly drop elevation down to lake level. Happily, I have the entire place to myself - apparently the big group are camping elsewhere tonight. I'm so exhausted I can barely cook dinner while sitting on the ground.

After dinner I set up my tent in a rain and sleet mix before crawling inside to escape the weather. I'm wet, muddy and exhausted. Pulling off my boots reveals large bloodstains on both socks. Damn.

My old leather hiking boots are falling apart and now rub on my heels and toes in multiple places. I'm only on day three and still have a long way to go. This is not good. I eat two Oreos to cheer up before fixing my feet - wash, dry, disinfect, band-aid and dry socks.
When finished I eat another Oreo to cheer up.
Then I eat two more.
My Oreo ration for tomorrow is gone.

Day 4 - 1,650ft. up / 660ft. down / 7.5 hrs

During the night I wake multiple times to heavy rain, though happily my tent is in good shape and keeps me and my gear dry. When I finally emerge I'm greeted by an overcast morning that blocks any view of the massive mountains I know surround me. Still feeling tired and down about my feet, I opt for a slow start. Relaxing while enjoying breakfast is a nice change, and I feel well rested when I leave camp at 8am.

Immediately I hike into a deep valley lined with extremely active glaciers. The far wall has ice continually moving and breaking, making for the most active ice I have ever seen and heard. The constant cracking and avalanches are at first very disconcerting, and I flinch every time I hear what sounds like gunshots. Loud booms echo off the narrow valley walls, and each avalanche sounds like a jet flying low overhead.

As the morning turns to afternoon I slowly grow accustomed to the booming sounds and eventually feel comforted by them. I move past a duo of gorgeous aqua-marine lakes (*Lagunas Siula* and *Quesillococha*) to the highest pass on the hike so far (15,840ft.).

At the end of the valley the trail takes a serious turn uphill, and I immediately slow to a crawl. I am sure even snails move faster than me, though I'm proud to be only five minutes behind the large group. The clouds have burned off and the view continues to improve the higher I climb, providing the perfect excuse to stop and take photos. From the summit I have mind-blowing views of the enormous mountains at the heart of the range - *Yerupajá* (21,892ft.) and mighty *Siula Grande* (20,814ft.).

I find a beautiful sheltered and sunny spot on lush green grass and am thankful for a break from the biting icy wind. My little perch has a million dollar view and is a great spot to eat my raw Mr. Noodle. I thoroughly enjoy taking my time, soaking in the food, warm sunshine and expansive views.

After prying myself away I slowly move down to *Huayhuash Campsite* for a 3.30pm arrival. I can almost hike at my normal pace on flat ground, though I'm still painfully slow up and downhill. I thoroughly warm up and dry out in the afternoon sun at camp, boosting my morale. Lounging on the grass I'm awed when three quarters of the sky turns orange and red in a magical display at sunset.
A quick check and cleanup before bed reveals my feet have not deteriorated since yesterday.

Day 5 - 1,650ft. up / 1,320ft. down / 5 hrs

Again I wake to imposing low cloud and overcast skies, making me feel groggy and lazy. I'm shocked to see visibility is reduced to twenty yards, giving an extremely eerie feeling to camp. Without direct sun in the early morning I'm soon cold, so I pack up and get moving by 7am. In good spirits and good time I cruise up the pass for the day - *Portachuelo de Huayhuash*, 15,675ft. It's blowing a gale on the summit and snowing lightly, causing me to quickly lose feeling in my hands and face - which I take as a sign not to linger.

At midday I arrive at the hot springs campsite in light rain, and force myself to set up the tent before a soak. The drizzle and cold air combine for a sublime soak and the mountain views don't hurt either. I soak all afternoon in the massive concrete pool, feeling content to do absolutely nothing in the perfectly hot water.

Late in the afternoon I explore the entire valley, stepping among numerous hot vents and creeks. An enormous volume of hot water flows from the ground here, and I take great pleasure in each new hot discovery.

Spread over a few hundred square feet I find more than a hundred sources of hot water before I stop really looking. In multiple places algae and tufa has formed in beautiful shades of green, red and orange.

I return to the soaking tub and spend the afternoon daydreaming about the amazing soaking options nearby that don't involve ugly concrete tubs.

After dinner I return to soak, thoroughly enjoying stretching out my legs. When I finally find the courage and dash to my tent, I discover it's a late night, much later than any other on this hike - 10pm! I crawl into my sleeping bag already toasty warm for the first time in a long time, and fall instantly into a deep sleep. At only five hours, this has been a short, easy day. I feel good!

Day 6 - 1,730ft. up / 1,650ft. down / 5 hrs

The hot spring lures me from the tent at 6am, and I'm extremely excited to see blue sky in all directions. I want to get moving quickly, knowing what is in store for today. Of course, there is always time to soak in a hot spring, so I do just that before breakfast and a quick pack up. I'm on the trail at 7:10am, moving slow and steady to *Punta Cuyoc* at 16,500ft., the highest point on the hiking circuit. With no wind, I'm able to thoroughly enjoy the expansive views from the top.

Resting on the summit, I realize I'm feeling much better. My feet are not bothering me, and the pain in my back and legs has receded to a dull ache. I can almost ignore them now. Eating half the food in my pack has made it much lighter than on day one. Altogether, I'm moving well - on the uphill sections I only stop for short rests now.

My goal for today is *Mirador San Antonio*, the best viewpoint to see the mighty *Siula Grande* close up. Unfortunately clouds roll in by the time I reach the side trail to the lookout, causing me to hesitate. I have literally dreamed of this view for years and so I want to do it justice with clear skies. Realizing how important it is to me, I decide on the spot to cut the day short and camp right where I am. I will get up early and power to the lookout with fresh legs and hopefully clear skies.

This makes for another short, easy day and I feel good lazing in the late afternoon sunshine. The temperature drops rapidly when the sun dips below the mountains and I begin to worry how cold the night will be. I camp alone on the alpine meadow where I can see for miles in every direction. Quickly I feel the enormous solitude, and dive into the warmth of my tent after stargazing for as long as I can tolerate the cold.

Day 7 - 5,610ft. up / 4,450ft. down / 9 hrs

I wake repeatedly in the night, unable to sleep because I'm so cold. Before first light I lie awake for an hour hugging myself for warmth, and am relieved to finally see daylight brighten the tent. Excited for the day ahead, I quickly make breakfast and pack up, despite the lack of feeling in my fingers. I skip away from my makeshift campsite at 6:40am, elated to see clear skies all around. Camping alone to wait for clear skies has paid off.

In an attempt to thoroughly warm up, I hike double-speed to the base of the climb, which also succeeds in waking me fully. I stash my pack behind a wall of rock and begin the steep uphill scramble to the lookout. Free of my pack I feel like an explorer on the moon, virtually bouncing off the ground with each step. Although the climb is steep and rocky, I find it easy without my pack dragging me down.

I take the last few steps to the top of the lookout and am utterly staggered by what I see. I feel as if the enormous mountains are right in front of me, close enough to reach out and touch. I continually scamper back and forward along the ridge, taking in the view from every possible angle.

When I read *Touching The Void* as a teenager in Australia I had no idea I would one day be at the very mountain, above the infamous valley. I used to think to myself 'I wish I could go there', but would soon put it out of my mind. I genuinely believed such a thing was impossible for an average guy like me. I struggle to comprehend that I'm really at the scene of the accident.
It really is possible to make dreams come true.

I linger as long as possible, soaking in the view and unable to stop grinning broadly.

Knowing I face a long day, I half run, half slide down the scree slope and am relived to see my undisturbed pack. It now weighs roughly what I normally hike with so I can move at my usual fast pace on flat ground. Only now I'm moving well do I realize my previous snail's pace has been hurting my morale.

My usual plan for hiking with a heavy pack is to move fast whenever it's actually on my back in an effort to wear it for the shortest time possible. I have always felt I'm actively getting more exhausted every minute the heavy pack is on my back, even when standing still. Now that I can finally move fast again I will be less exhausted, because the pack is on my back for less hours per day.

The trail meets a small river and twists and turns with the shore for a few miles. I decide to stay on the right-hand bank, though an hour later it's clear I have made the wrong decision. The river shoots over an impressive waterfall, with no path down on the right. On the far bank I can clearly see a well-worn series of boulders acting as steps. A little upstream I fight the underbrush to the river's edge, about five yards wide and seething whitewater. I search up and down for almost thirty minutes, hoping to find a safe crossing. With my heavy pack making me unstable I don't feel confident hopping across the huge boulders in the river as I normally would. Eventually I settle on a crossing that will just have to do and I get a huge adrenaline rush as I go for it, leaping from boulder to boulder. I lean forward and let the momentum of my pack push me forward and across. The crossing has cost almost an hour, though the views as I climb down the waterfall make up for it.

Soon after midday I skirt around the edge of *Huayllapa*, the only village on the trail. It's possible to buy supplies here, though after thinking about it for ten minutes, I feel certain I don't need anything. I also resist the temptation to buy a coke or fried food - both favourites of mine while hiking. In an attempt to get away from town, I continue without stopping. After studying the map I estimate an hour of climbing to the campsite where I plan to eat lunch.

On the edge of town the trail takes a savage turn uphill, climbing through endless switchbacks. I push on and on, my energy falling with each step. I continually think about stopping for lunch, though I'm convinced camp is just over the next rise. I'm utterly exhausted when I finally arrive two and a half hours later, foot sore and ravenous.

This has been by far the hardest day yet, and I don't even have the energy to stumble around camp for photos. I lamely sit on the ground beside my tent for two hours while eating lunch raw then cooking and eating dinner. I am so beaten and miserable even the hot food fails to cheer me up and so I climb into bed long before sunset. Before I stuff my feet into clean socks I see they are wet and worse than ever. The raw skin is so soft it has not healed at all.
My old hiking boots are in tatters.

Day 8 - 1,650ft. up / 3,950ft. down / 7.5 hrs

I'm again freezing overnight and lie awake for hour after hour, not warm enough to sleep. Finally, sick of lying around, I get up at the first hint of light and make an attempt to take photos and explore the area. It feels good to stretch my legs without my pack, and I feel better for moving.

I push hard and move past the first pass of the day, *Punta Tapuish*, 15,840ft. in good time. I cross a beautiful lush green valley and climb to the second pass *Punta Yaucha*, 15,975ft., still moving well. I'm a little confused to have two passes in one day, and I'm not entirely certain this is the right way. Normally this would be utterly exhausting, though today I'm flying. The trail is less steep and my pack is lighter than ever, so I move quickly and easily. I'm finally able to keep up with the suggested times from a guide book, something to be proud of.

I eat lunch on top of the pass, trying hard to soak in the immense views. I linger and realize I'm not ready for this day to end. I slowly descend into a lush valley to the familiar campsite at *Laguna Yahuacocha* - my campsite from day one. It's hard to believe this is my last night on the trail. Even with two passes, today has been easy. I feel strong and my feet are more or less the same.

Throughout the hike the large group of Israelis has been shadowing me and we have shared many campsites. Their guide Ernesto speaks only Spanish, while none of the Israelis do. Because I'm always quick to say hello and ask how he is doing, we have struck up a friendship during the hike. For this last night Ernesto gives me popcorn and french fries he has made for the tourists, and I practically kiss him with my thanks. The two of us chat back and forth about many things, eventually coming around to money, work, and the Western World.

I feel sad when he explains how little he is paid to guide this group. I know each tourist has paid hundreds of dollars to a large company, which then pays Ernesto peanuts.

"Do you know how much they pay?" I ask, nodding towards the tourists who are each staring into an iPhone.
"No."
"Do you *want* to know?" I ask after a pause.
"No," he quickly replies, sadness in his eyes.
Ernesto moves away, not wanting to meet my gaze.

Day 9 - 825ft. up / 3,300ft. down / 4.5 hrs

For the first time on the hike, I sleep like a baby, despite my useless sleeping pad. Maybe I'm finally used to it. After more photos, a quick goodbye to Ernesto and one last look around, I'm on the trail at my usual time of 7am. I stroll along easily and reach the pass in two and a half hours. There is no rush today. I find a slightly different trail to take down to *Llamac*, which only takes two more hours. A wide trail and distinct lack of cacti makes me think this is the actual trail, and the way I should have hiked up on the first day. It would be been nice to avoid that cacti...

I immediately check and am happy to see the Jeep is perfectly safe and untouched. Sitting on the ground next to it I eat a final victory Oreo and buy a bag of chips and a half-frozen can of Coke, half of which sprays out when I open it.
The hard ground makes me realize how much I'm looking forward to patching the hole in my sleeping pad.

Being alone in the wilderness and pushing my limits has again been extremely difficult, and extremely rewarding.

I'm exhausted and jubilant at the same time.

Modern Day Slavery

Potosi, Bolivia
November 2010

W AGES in Latin America are vastly different than in The
Developed World. It's common to earn less than $5 USD
for twelve hours of hard labor. That in itself is not a terrible
thing - when food and the basics of life are also extremely
cheap, everything balances out. What shocks and sickens me,
however, is exploitation by global corporations on an enormous
scale. These corporations post multi-billion dollar profits on
the back of slave labor.

Across Latin America this was most obvious in the world's
highest city, *Potosi*, in Bolivia at 13,400ft. The enormous
Cerro Rico (Rich Mountain) dominates the skyline and is
visible from virtually every street corner, which makes sense
given it is single-handedly responsible for the very existence of
Potosi. Centuries ago, the native peoples knew the mountain

was bursting with precious metals. They mined huge quantities of the highest quality silver and other valuable ores over many generations.

With the arrival of the Spanish *conquistadors* the rate of removal was stepped up to a staggering scale. At the high point, 3,600lbs of pure Silver was being extracted every single day! The silver was mined by forced slave labor and immediately shipped to Spain to increase the crown's wealth. Over the centuries the mountain has been mined so heavily that almost nothing remains. Today thousands of man hours are required for a pitiful haul.

To get a better understanding of the situation, I sign up for a mine tour with Miguel and Carlos, locals and former miners themselves. After ten years of back-breaking work, these guys saw there was no future. They simply had to find a path to a better life, or surrender to the misery. In the evenings, they taught themselves English and eventually became tour guides for a large foreign-owned tourist company. Having recently started their own tour company, Miguel and Carlos are extremely excited to finally be working for themselves.

With a few hours to kill, I hang around their small office, and eventually help translate their brochure into better English. I sense they are happy to meet a foreigner who speaks Spanish and actually cares about what's going on. After lots of chatter, Miguel and Carlos invite me to a local soccer match. *Potosi* is playing a nearby city at the stadium tonight, and the crowd alone will be entertaining, they say. I jump at the chance to hangout with locals, always looking for a way to see the world through their eyes.

In the early evening I find Miguel and Carlos and together we amble towards the stadium. Moving closer, we're swept up in a wave of rowdy people already moving in that direction. I'm amused to see scalpers, and after some heavy negotiating we buy tickets from one for just over face value. Miguel says we are lucky to get tickets last minute like this and clearly does not care at all about the tiny price premium. In the meantime, Carlos has made another important purchase - a hip flask of whiskey each.

"Hide these," says Carlos as he passes me all three bottles with a wink. At the entrance gate Carlos and Miguel are thoroughly patted down for contraband and weapons, while I'm waved straight through - apparently because I'm a foreigner.

Of course, we all grin like idiots.

The soccer match is fast-paced and high-skill, and around five thousand people cheer like mad in the modern stadium. Supporters from both sides have decided to sit together on one side, making things very interesting. Inevitably, the crowd becomes very, very rowdy. At one point a serious yelling match breaks out, before escalating into shoving from both sides. While it looks serious, I don't actually see any punches thrown.

While sneaking sips of whiskey, I ask Miguel if we have anything to worry about.
"Only if you cheer for the other team," he says with a wink and a grin.

Ψ   Ψ   Ψ

Sporting a small headache in the morning, I wander across town with a potent coffee. The group I will be touring the mine with are milling around and Miguel, Carlos and I nod knowingly at each other, thick as thieves about our antics last night. They are in their element here, giving orders and herding visitors in the right direction. I'm excited as we gear-up with weather-proof layers in preparation for entering the mine. This includes waterproof outer layers, huge gumboots, helmets and headlamps - all of which has me sweating profusely.

Now ready to go, we move across town to the miner's market, a district of town where mining essentials are sold. It's tradition for visitors to purchase gifts for the men working that day, so we search the shelves looking for the perfect items. Common gifts are dynamite for blasting, coca leaves for chewing and sugary soda to wash it down.

I'm amused to see anyone can buy cheap sticks of dynamite with no questions asked. I briefly consider buying a few to keep for special occasions, though think better of it - surely it will only lead to trouble. Again there are no questions asked when we buy coca leaves, the raw ingredient cocaine is made from. Chewing the leaves gives a similar buzz, which many people find energizing. I have chewed the leaves a few times in South America, and I personally just get a small buzz similar to an extremely strong coffee. Chewing the leaves for an entire day is said to result in a person never feeling tired. I have never warmed to the taste enough to test this theory.

As soon as we step into the silver refinery I feel as if we have stepped back in time. On display are textbook mineral refinery equipment and techniques from the 1750's. Raw rock is crushed with extremely noisy and dangerous machinery before being refined with a variety of potent chemicals. A raw paste is created consisting of mostly lead and a small amount of silver. None of the massive crushing machines have any safety devices or guards, and none of the workers wear eye or ear protection despite the thundering racket. The dust in the air is gritty in my teeth, and the chemicals burn my nose and eyes. Miguel says working in the refinery is comparatively easy, which I find hard to believe.

As we move closer the mountain is imposing, and I feel it has a supernatural quality like so many fictional mountains. An enormous horizontal shaft has been dug directly into the side, serving as the entrance. We walk along the shaft, following a small gauge train track. I smash my head on the low roof repeatedly after only a hundred yards making me thankful for my helmet. We stop roughly half a mile in, where the harsh environment starts to show it's ugly head. The heat, humidity and dust combined are nauseating. All of this combined with the high elevation means there is virtually no oxygen to actually breathe. What little air my lungs can get is stale and thick with pulverized rock.

Carlos explains the mine is a giant cooperative run by the locals themselves. They work together to maintain the refinery, and occasionally hold group work days where the shared main shaft and train tracks are built and maintained. These costs are deducted from whatever they can manage to find.

Miguel leads us into a small side tunnel where the humidity and dust increase ten fold. When my eyes adjust to the dim light cast by my head lamp, I see young men chipping at the rock face with hand tools. I watch as one young man holds a chisel while another swings a large sledge hammer. With each forceful blow a tiny fragment of rock is chipped off, which another young boy carefully gathers into a small pile. Progress is excruciatingly slow.

I crawl on my belly through a tiny hole in the rock, barely able to wriggle forward, before I emerge into a rock chamber roughly half the size of my Jeep. Here, an older man is using a large sledge hammer and round chisel to 'drill' a hole in the rock. He is working in an extremely tight space, with only ten inches to swing the sledge. With each swing he issues a genuine grunt from the exertion before rotating the chisel and swinging again. He is sweating profusely and in between deep breaths says it will take six hours to drill each dynamite hole.

Once he has 'drilled' six holes, dynamite will be placed into each hole and blasted to remove more rock. After the struggle to get in I'm extremely short on air, sweating profusely and uncomfortable. For the first time in my life I feel claustrophobic and have to force myself to concentrate and calm down. My skin feels clammy and I'm breathing rapidly and much too shallow to actually get any oxygen in. I have never had a panic attack, though I start to understand what it must feel like.

The older man is related to everyone working here and is only fifty-five, he tells me. He has been working in the mine for over thirty-five years, for ten to twelve hours a day, six or seven days a week. His sixteen year old son is the young man in the next chamber collecting small fragments of rock by hand. Their brothers, uncles and cousins are all scattered around, chipping, digging and gathering rock. They have been in the mine for eight hours already today, and will probably work another four, he says.

Because of the heat, humidity and dust, none of them eat any food during the long day. Chewing coca leaves and drinking sugary soda is their only nutrition. While watching them labor for ten minutes in these unbearable conditions, I'm struck by the realization these men will do this for the rest of their lives. I get to leave in fifteen minutes, they do not.

Seeing the sixteen year old boy working in these conditions is distressing. These miners expect to live until around fifty, when they will be overcome by lung and respiratory problems. That is if they are lucky enough to avoid mine collapses and the many other risks associated with life underground.

The combination of shock and sorrow I feel for this family is overwhelming, and I immediately give them all my dynamite and coco leaves.
I wish I had more.

Ψ   Ψ   Ψ

Back in the main shaft we stop at a statue of The Virgin Mary where the miners make a daily toast for good luck. We each take a small sip from a bottle being passed around and I'm bewildered to see the bottle is identical to the one I bought to burn in my camp stove. We're toasting with 99% rubbing alcohol - and the miners do this every day.

Carlos explains the miners commonly work in a tight family unit and earn roughly fifty cents an hour each. From this tiny wage they must buy all their mining supplies, support their families, and attempt to enjoy what little life they have outside the mine. Carlos goes on to say the men we visited are good friends of his, and his immediate family are in a nearby chamber laboring away at the rock face.

I'm relieved when we break out into warm sunshine, and I take many deep breaths of the fresh air. The sun stings my eyes and I am thankful for it.

Miguel explains the raw paste leaving the refinery is sold to a Peruvian company for pennies. The price is marked up ten fold before being sold to an American company. This company again marks up the price ten fold before selling it on the global market. This is the silver used to make the electronics and jewelry we buy in department stores.

It hits me like a ton of bricks.
The reason you and I can buy an iPhone or TV so cheaply is because these men are literally working themselves to death in this mine. They earn one hundred times less than the accepted global price for the silver while doing so.
In The Developed World we don't have slaves in our houses, but we absolutely still have slaves working for us - and they are working to an early grave.
You and I have simply moved our slaves out of sight and mind.

Ψ   Ψ   Ψ

For a final bang, Miguel and Carlos take out a stick of dynamite. I'm impressed to see it looks exactly like I expect and it feels like soft clay. A detonator and fuse are inserted and the whole thing is packed in a bag of ammonium nitrate to increase the power of the explosion. When they light the fuse, everyone surges back, though I move forward, eager to hold the dynamite with fuse furiously burning down.

After thirty seconds of fun, Carlos runs down the hill to throw the dynamite package on the ground before running back in plenty of time before the explosion.

Even fifty yards away, the shock wave is strong enough to knock the air out of my lungs!

The Uyuni Salt Flats

Bolivian Altiplano
November 2010

P REPARING to leave *Uyuni* in Southern Bolivia, I feel like
we're setting out on a mission to Mars. We're attempting
to venture further into the unknown that ever before. Traipsing
around town for two days organizing and reorganizing gear has
been an expedition in itself and the sheer amount of supplies
we must collect seems fit for a small army. We have also been
trying our best to get and any and all information about our
planned route and chances of success.
I sense we have absolutely no idea what lies ahead.

Ψ   Ψ   Ψ

I'm determined to explore the Uyuni Salt Flats of Bolivia
and beyond, which means venturing far off the beaten track,
deep into the unknown. To increase safety and the chances of

success, more vehicles are ideal, so I'm teaming up with other Overlanders. A few days ago I met Warren and Sara who are driving an old Toyota 4Runner. Originally from the UK, they flew to California to buy the Toyota and are having the time of their lives on a similar journey to mine. Living in the extremely cramped confines of a little 4x4 has pushed their relationship to the limit, run-of-the-mill for Overlanding couples. I gather they often give each other the silent treatment for days at a time. The battered Toyota has suffered a host of mechanical problems, only increasing the stress and tension between them.

Months ago Warren and Sarah met Rob, a larger than life American riding a motorbike on a similar journey. Rob had a major crash in Peru in few months ago, and was flown back to the US for surgery on his leg. Now back on the road, he is chomping at the bit for new adventures. From the moment I meet Rob, I sense a gentle giant. He always has a broad smile plastered on his face, and nothing is a problem or concern. Laid back and easy going, I know immediately Rob and I will be friends. For reasons I don't quite understand, Rob is riding a classic Harley Davidson.
Yes, that's right. A Harley Davidson. With street tires and three inches of ground clearance.

We form a motley crew, thrown together by chance and a shared goal.

Our mission is to drive across the spectacular *Salar de Uyuni* (Uyuni Salt Flats) in remote Southern Bolivia. From there, we will continue South through the mighty *Atacama* desert, hopefully all the way into Chile. We are well aware of the enormity of the task - many hundreds of miles on virtually non-existent roads in the harshest of conditions. Added to this, the best maps we can find are woefully inadequate. I am certain adventure will find us one way or another.

Walking around town I ask everyone with a vehicle for more information about our planned route, hoping to glean precious details. My questions are met with interesting if not cryptic responses. I ask which tracks we must take (*the biggest ones*), how far we need to travel gas-wise (*something around 300 to 500 miles*) and if we will make it on our own (*maybe, maybe not*). I'm told we will find virtually no human habitation, and the chances of assistance are virtually nil. There is absolutely no gas, food or water available on our planned route. This information reinforces the seriousness of what we are attempting, though isn't actually very useful.

We each load as much food and drinking water as we can carry, planning at least a week without resupply. Of course I buy extra popcorn, quickly becoming my favourite after dinner snack on the road. I do my best to impart the seriousness of our undertaking on the crew, though I worry they are not taking it seriously enough. On multiple occasions I ask Rob if he will have enough gas to travel the required distance, and he assures me he does. When I run the numbers myself, I am unconvinced. Trying to talk this through gets me nowhere. Warren seems unconcerned about the many recent breakdowns suffered by his 4Runner, and is satisfied with his stash of tools and spare parts consisting of little more than wire and duct tape.

While working our way through town, we make a stop at the bustling central market for lunch. Here we order huge bowls of deliciously hot and spicy soup with big chunks of meat. The large bones are difficult to identify, and we ponder what we're actually eating. Only when we have all finished does the smiling lady tell us we have just eaten llama. Sheepishly, this beautifully dressed lady explains she was afraid to tell us before, concerned we would refuse to eat it. Only now do I notice the other stallholders intently watching our every reaction. In reality, the tender chunks are tasty and the hot soup is full of hearty vegetables. The face of our host lights up when we say as much in Spanish and Rob and I order a second steaming bowl to the delight of the onlookers.

For our final stop we pull into the only gas station in town, planning to fill everything to the brim. Gas and diesel are very cheap in Bolivia, though there is an official policy whereby foreigners pay double the advertised price. So far each of us has avoided this policy by visiting multiple stations and sweet-talking the attendants. Here in *Uyuni* there is no other station, and with all of us together and the Harley rumbling loudly, we attract attention wherever we go. As expected, we're asked to pay the foreigner price.

After much discussion it's clear the attendant has made this decision based on our foreign license plates and nothing else. Warren cleverly points out we could park off to the side and fill up containers for the regular price. We could then pour the gas into our foreign vehicles and avoid the price hike.

The attendant reluctantly agrees this is correct, and then realizes the conundrum. If we fill via containers, we will annoy him for the next two hours buying five gallons at a time. The people in line are already getting impatient, beeping horns and coming to investigate the hold-up. Clearly wanting to move on, the attendant relents and agrees to fill the vehicles at regular price.

For the first time on the entire trip I carry a five gallon jerrycan. Expecting deep sand, rocks and possibly mud, I know the Jeep will consume more than usual. The total distance to our goal and the next gas is uncertain, and I would rather be on the safe side. While filling the Jeep I rock it from side to side in an attempt to get every possible drop in. I'm certain I'll need all of the twenty-four gallons I'm now carrying. Likewise, the others fill to their maximum capacity.

We hit the road, happy to finally leave town and get underway. After only a few minutes we're surrounded by small sand dunes, scrubby bush and little else. It's ten miles to the edge of the *Salar*, and I'm surprised to see we're on our own so soon. There are no houses or huts and the track is extremely rough and appears virtually unused. It's dusty, sandy and slow going, and yet each of us is grinning from ear to ear. We think we understand what lies ahead, and we hope we are prepared.

En route to the entrance point onto the *Salar* at *Colchani* I am stunned to see an emu and chicks.
Yes, really. An emu.
In Bolivia.
Things are taking a bizarre turn, and we're not even on the salt yet.

We've been told repeatedly the most dangerous part of driving on the salt is actually getting on and off. With even a little rain the region between dirt and salt turns into a muddy salty slop, where vehicles quickly sink to their axles. The deep muck in all directions prevents other vehicles helping with extraction, and stricken vehicles are often stuck for days. With this in mind we tentatively follow the most heavily used tracks one at a time, leaving plenty of space between. After negotiating a few small puddles, we're soon rolling on smooth, solid salt and I'm relieved to clear the first hurdle without incident.

There is nothing on the horizon as far as I can see. Perfectly white, flat salt stretches far into the distance - it looks endless. Even in the late morning the sun beats down, reflecting harshly. There is not a single trace of life on the salt and the lunar-like landscape bares no resemblance to anything I have ever seen on this planet.

The surface is solid and flat, without cracks, lumps or soft spots. At first it appears smooth like concrete, though on closer inspection I see it's not entirely flat. The salt has formed into small hexagonal shapes on the surface that have slightly raised edges. I assume there is some natural process at work to cause the salt to form these perfectly uniform shapes. The quarter-inch raised edges of these hexagons are soft salt crystals which easily flatten when walked or driven on.

Black tire marks indicate the most heavily travelled directions, resembling 'roads' across the white nothing. They make for an easy-to-follow track, and allow me to re-establish my bearings whenever I venture away. Following the tire tracks feels limiting, so I continually veer off to explore every which way. It's difficult not to drive like a lunatic with the other vehicles so close and many cameras at the ready. The temptation is too great, and we all have a riot weaving huge slalom turns, and even a few high speed circles for no good reason. Never before have I driven on a surface that allows so much freedom. There is absolutely nothing for hundreds of miles.

Once away from the edge of the *Salar*, the view in all directions is identical. Flat. White. Solid. Salt.
I can see nothing else.

Stopping repeatedly for photos I'm awe-struck by the alien landscape. Just for fun, I walk a few hundred yards away from the Jeep while my companions continue on. Quickly I feel an overwhelming sense of isolation and vulnerability. I genuinely feel uncomfortable to be alone out here, so huge is the landscape.

After re-joining the team, we consult our basic maps together. Using my compass, I'm fairly certain which tracks we need to follow, so we aim for *Incahuasi Island* with ear-to-ear grins plastered across our faces.

The 'island' is actually a huge chunk of regular old dirt and rocks jutting out of the salt. When it materializes on the horizon through the shimmering heat-mirage I'm relieved I led us in the correct direction. Because it's so dark in color and has small trees and cacti, it looks exactly like a distant island in the ocean. With nothing nearby to judge scale, it's impossible to determine how far away or how big it is.

Being in no particular hurry to reach the island, we thoroughly enjoy investigating every irregularity and small curiosity we can find. The wind has steadily increased all day, and now late in the afternoon, it's extremely strong and oddly continuous. I feel as if there is a solid wall of wind, rather than the usual gusts. The door of the Jeep is violently torn from my hand whenever I open it and I have never seen the canvas sides deform inward so far. It's as if some unseen giant is leaning directly against them and I can only hope they will not be damaged by the onslaught.

We arrive at the island soon before sunset, and after driving a complete lap find a great place to camp on the protected lee side. I race to the top for sunset photos, and am shocked how quickly I struggle with the lack of oxygen. On the flat salt with no mountains in sight I have completely forgotten I'm at an elevation of 12,000 feet. The wind is bitingly cold, so I barely last five minutes on the summit before my hands are so numb I'm forced to scramble back down.

The clear night provides spectacular star gazing and is staggeringly cold, forcing me to bury deep into my sleeping bag. Before sunrise I pull every drawstring in an attempt to conserve what precious little heat I can.

Ψ   Ψ   Ψ

Sunrise over camp is spectacular, and thankfully the wind has completely blown itself out. I discover small chunks of ice in all my water bottles, confirming just how cold it was overnight. We drink multiple cups of steaming coffee, trying to comprehend the bizarre view over the salt while soaking in the warm sun. Soon there is plenty of stupidity and laughter while experimenting with forced perspective photos using all the props we can find. Because there is nothing to give any size or distance perspective in the vast whiteness, it's easy to make objects look disproportionately tiny or huge, similar to being on the moon. I stand close to the camera while the Jeep is far away, and the resulting photo is normal size me standing next to a tiny Jeep. With nothing for scale reference, it's impossible to tell I'm not standing next to the Jeep.

It's great to have so many hours to soak in the alien landscape - every few minutes we go silent, simply staring around, still disbelieving. Even early in the morning the sun is harsh, and my skin is already raw from the biting wind. Throwing the frisbee on the salt is fantastic, there is never anything to trip over.

Reluctantly, we move South.

With the island fading in my mirrors, I think about a top speed run in the Jeep. I have always wondered how fast it can go and it would be fun to drive faster than ever before. After 70mp/h I think better of the idea. I simply can not bring myself to push the little Jeep to it's limit. She has been so good to me, I like to be kind to her in return. On top of that I need to conserve gas and there really is no point.

After driving more than a hundred miles and twenty-four hours on continuous salt, it's disorienting when a black line appears through the heat haze - the edge of the salt. To exit, we navigate another series of small tracks, a combination of dry mud, sand and dirt. From the second we leave the salt we are on extremely dusty and corrugated gravel tracks, which vanish repeatedly. Soon I doubt the existence of a road at all.

Our maps are proving woefully inadequate, leaving me uncertain of which track to take. All I have is a general idea of the direction we must go, based on my compass. With little other option, as a group we follow whatever track appears most used. Every few miles the surface changes, keeping us on our toes and forcing us to concentrate. It changes between deep sand, rock slabs, powder-fine dust, shallow river crossings and the occasional small salt flat. We never see another vehicle.

Soon Rob is sweating profusely, working hard to keep the monster Harley upright. Rob is a big guy - over six foot five and 230lbs - and is using every ounce of strength in the deep sandy ruts. Rob rides in front to avoid the thick dust we create, and so we can keep an eye on him. I watch helplessly from the Jeep as he battles time and time again, fighting the weaving and bucking monster.

Inevitably, the enormous bike crashes down. We have most of Rob's gear in the Jeep, though in the deep sand the Harley is still too heavy to pick up single handedly. Warren and I dash over to lend a hand, trying to help share Rob's burden - even a little.

Despite Rob's best efforts, the Harley topples repeatedly in the deep sand. In response, Warren and I develop a rhythm whereby whoever is closer jumps out to assist. A few times the Harley gets beached on the home-made skid plate, now stuffed with sand. At these times it takes all three of us to even budge the monster.

Following the most obvious track and trusting the compass we miraculously find the tiny village of *San Juan* in the early afternoon. It's comprised of a handful of small buildings and a general store, making for a great rest stop. Briefly we consider calling it a day, though we're all eager to find a wild campsite in the expansive landscape.

Just twenty minutes from town the Harley repeatedly loses power, eventually coughing to a stop and refusing to start. Warren, Rob and I put our heads together, but can not think of an explanation. We speculate the problem may be bad gas, or something electrical. The modern Harley has computer-controlled fuel injection, and we hope like mad this is not the cause. Checking for gas and spark at every opportunity, we slowly dismantle the bike over the course of an hour. Eventually, we find and tighten a loose battery connector. The monster roars again with a new lease on life.

Sunset has long ago come and gone and the wind has again built to an insane level. The temperature has plummeted, and standing outside is now unbearably cold. With the bike fixed, I suddenly realize just how cold and exhausted I am. I put on all of my thermal layers under many more clothes, though my extremities remain numb for half an hour. Later I discover a bad case of windburn on my arms, face and legs. Standing on the exposed roadside dealing with Rob's bike took it's toll.

At a quick team meeting we agree we're all freezing and exhausted. It's also now pitch black and getting colder by the second, so it's an easy decision to turn back to *San Juan*. We manage to find a small hotel - little more than a concrete box - where we negotiate beds for the night for a few dollars each. We're relieved the building is surrounded by a rock wall, the perfect windbreak. We can barely keep our eyes open while cooking pasta on our camp stoves and chatting about our day.

Ψ   Ψ   Ψ

The morning is crisp and clear, thankfully without wind again. After breakfast we take the opportunity to look over our respective vehicles and make adjustments to gear. I pour the jerrycan into the main tank and hope it will be enough. On the advice of our host, we leave town in a different direction than yesterday afternoon. We place our trust in local knowledge rather than our basic maps.

The small salt flat of *Chiguana* is a relief after the corrugated gravel, allowing us to travel at forty miles an hour on even the worst parts. It's great fun to again drive next to each other, play around taking photos and be reckless. On the Southern edge we stumble into the tiny town of the same name, comprised of a few mud huts and sticks. After posing for photos with the heavily armed Military we turn South on their advice. Immediately we're on a tiny track that is clearly seldom driven. The track is so small Rob stops for a team meeting, and we're all feeling uneasy about the directions we have been given. With little choice, we continue on, hoping this track will go somewhere useful.

A handful of miles later we're left with little doubt we have entered a genuine desert. Huge sand dunes and bizarre rock formations rise above us on all sides. The track weaves around the biggest of these, while going directly over and through the smaller obstacles. Towering barren mountains loom high above in the near distance. There is absolutely no vegetation of any kind. The baking sun is relentless, and I'm forced to put a towel over my arm in attempt to avoid sunburn. I can only imagine how Rob must be overheating, wearing thick black leathers.

I'm always confident in my map and compass skills, and I feel good about navigating our team. The 20,000 foot peaks surrounding us correspond nicely with my map, increasing my confidence. When we arrive at the sizable town of *Copacabaña*, confusion sets in. After ten minutes staring at the map, I am forced to admit I am completely lost. When I try to guess North without looking at the compass, I point due South. Not for the first time in Bolivia I am utterly disoriented. Normally my built in compass is reliable, and I stupidly begin to doubt the compass in my hand.

To my knowledge, *Copacabaña* is not on any map, and I still have no idea where it is. Again we place our trust in locals, and leave town in a new direction, still feeling uncertain. The desert feels larger still.

We're now driving on bright red dirt, in and around strange rock towers. It's clear we're again on tracks that are seldom driven, and we still have not seen a single vehicle. Having lost all confidence in my navigation skills, I conclude we must be on tracks not marked on my maps. I therefore have absolutely no idea where we are, and put away the map and compass.

Late in the day we stumble upon the spectacular *Laguna Hedionda*, packed with flamingos. There are many large pink ones and also smaller white flamingos and I'm shocked to learn they only turn pink after years of eating small crustaceans from the water. We find a few tiny abandoned rock huts near the shore which we hope will provide enough protection from the frigid wind again whipping up dust.

For the first time on the entire journey, I seriously consider sleeping inside the Jeep due to the brutally cold wind. After moving gear I try to lie down before concluding it just isn't big enough. I struggle to pitch my tent in the lee of the Jeep without it blowing away. My companions have a similar struggle, attempting to find whatever protection they can. While cooking dinner, the sand whipped up by the relentless wind gets the better of us all and fraying nerves are pushed to the limit.

I become fixated on my tub of honey, a spoon of which in a cup of tea has become my favourite luxury item. Overnight it froze solid, making me very unhappy. I'm so exhausted and fixated on a cup of tea with honey, I spend almost an hour boiling the container in hot water. The plan works well enough and the steaming cups we share improves our collective mood. Not normally one to suffer such extreme mood swings, I realize the impact the harsh conditions are having on my state of mind.

Ψ   Ψ   Ψ

The temperature again plummets overnight and in the morning I'm not surprised to find all my water bottles inside the Jeep frozen solid. Under the hood the washer fluid reservoir is also rock solid. I hope it hasn't cracked. Soon after setting off in the early morning, Rob and I are separated from Warren and Sara. After I have not seen them in my mirror for ten minutes, I pull over to wait.

The tracks this morning have been deep rutted sand, and the Jeep works hard to push through. Thinking of how much gas I burn in the deep sand, I'm reluctant to backtrack. After waiting almost an hour, and with no other choice, I make the return trip of ten miles. Rob and I agree he should stay put, there is no reason for him to battle more sand than nessescarry. For the first time, I become hyper aware of my gas situation.

I eventually find Warren lying in the dirt under his Toyota - never a good sign. He is deeply concerned about oil dripping from the transfer case. Warren explains he scraped over a large rock yesterday, and is now worried about damage. We thoroughly wipe off all the oil before looking around with headlamps. After careful study we both agree it's just the breather venting a little oil, probably caused by the elevation and wild temperature swings. Feeling better about the Toyota, we move on to find Rob while keeping a close eye on things.

Ψ   Ψ   Ψ

The days begin to blur. We move from one flamingo-covered lake to the next, all while crossing sandy and rocky barren desert terrain. We hover around 15,000 feet in elevation, always surrounded by much higher mountains. We make stops at the famous 'rock tree', the stunning orange and white *Laguna Colorada* and camp next to a hot spring that we soak in for countless hours.

The nights are excruciatingly cold and the sun blazes during the day, causing ever increasing sun and windburn. The exhaustion and extreme elements slowly tear at each of us, and we're increasingly anxious about our dwindling food, drinking water and gas supplies.

Ψ   Ψ   Ψ

On the sixth and hopefully final day, we all hit our physical and mental limits. The last half gallon of drinking water is shared out, and all gas containers have been empty for days. The few locals we encounter living in stone huts are certain of the distance we have remaining, though none agree on that distance.

As predicted, Rob does not have enough gas to reach our destination. We toy with the idea of siphoning some from the Jeep, though in the end decide it's better for the bike to run out than the Jeep. Miraculously, Rob finds a man selling expensive and cloudy gas out of coke bottles. Rob has run out of Bolivian cash, so I lend him everything I have. With little gas, almost no drinking water and no money remaining, my options are quickly closing down.

Further South at the beautiful bright green *Laguna Verde*, the wind continues to tear at my ragged state of mind. I'm only able to stand outside for ten seconds - long enough for one photo - before diving back inside for shelter. The dust is so severe and fine everything inside the Jeep is coated in a fine layer - including me. My sunglasses become so heavily coated I'm forced to stop every ten minutes to clean them enough to see.

I become fixated on the enormous *Volcàn Licancahur* at 19,000ft., directly ahead. It sits at the far end of the stunning green lake, and I know it marks the border with Chile.
We have almost made it.

We each take a different line through the deep sand around the lake, and in the scramble the vehicles become separated from the motorbike. After waiting an eternity, I drive back, circling the entire lake searching. We have no idea if Rob is in front of us or behind and I really don't want to leave him stranded alone.

On the far side of the lake I can not find Rob or any tire tracks, so I'm forced to again re-trace my own tracks to Warren and Sara. At this, I completely lose it. I yell and scream and hit the steering wheel, furious about the twenty miles of gas wasted. Luckily, I'm alone in the Jeep and nobody sees my childish display.

With no choice we move forward and thirty minutes later find Rob waiting at the Chilean border. Filled with relief, we manage to grin and laugh about the mix up.
We're almost there.

Distant mountains frame a tiny isolated shack in the middle of nowhere, marking the International Border between Bolivia and Chile. Apparently, the shack is Immigration. The officer says there is no Customs here, it's about forty miles back across the desert. We must go there to hand in our vehicle paperwork, he says. Running low on money, food, water and most importantly gas, this is never going to happen. I tell the Immigration officer we will just leave our vehicle papers with him.

"No problem," he says while throwing them on a stack of identical papers.

Warren, Sara and Rob have already paid fifteen *Bolivianos* (about $2 USD) for an exit stamp when I ask for my usual receipt. This is where the trouble starts. The Immigration officer explains that unfortunately we can not keep a receipt because they must be sent to *La Paz*, the capital.

I'm tired, hungry, sunburnt and covered in dust. I'm in no mood for any South American bribery crap and I argue loudly for the next ten minutes. This is an official border crossing and there is no way I will pay cash without an official receipt. Further, I add, I watched at the Immigration office in *Uyuni* where tourists were stamped out on their way to this exact border. Nobody paid a cent there.

"Yeah, that's different," he says with a smile.
Sure it is.

The officer is asking for fifteen *Bolivianos*, and Rob points out he only paid twelve *Bolivianos*, everything he had. Of course, the Immigration officer accepted that happily. This is a sure sign of bribery - he will take whatever he can get. Armed with this knowledge I become even more determined not to pay and continue to argue loudly.

Finally he reluctantly stamps my passport before handing it back. I notice my tourist card does not get a hologram-equipped sticker, which might be missed when it arrives in *La Paz*.

While waiting for Rob to organize his gear I stew in the Jeep, wondering if that was a stupid thing to do. Because of my stubbornness, the officer could make trouble. He could easily throw away my Customs paperwork, or mess with my tourist card, or one of a hundred other bad scenarios. I realize I'm getting too big for my boots and arguing too much. Sooner or later it's bound to land me in hot water.

Next time I vow to keep my mouth shut and pay the $2 USD, reciept or no reciept.

Ψ   Ψ   Ψ

Crossing into Chile we're stunned into silence. I'm so shocked by the development I even stop to take photos of the excellent paved road. It's disorienting to see a road with well painted lines, distance markers, corner signs and even emergency stopping lanes for trucks. The other drivers even use turn signals and drive sensibly and safely. I have not seen this kind of road and driving in so many months I wonder if I'm hallucinating from exhaustion. The highway rolls downhill from the mountains to sea level and with each mile the gas gauge on the Jeep actually goes up, alleviating my prior stress.

We pull into Customs and Immigration before *San Pedro de Atacama* to get stamped into Chile and receive paperwork for our vehicles. Chile is strict about quarantine, so we sign a long and serious looking legal declaration before a cursory inspection. The officer immediately finds and confiscates both my popcorn and honey. I spent over an hour turning that honey back into liquid, and feel a sense of loss watching it disappear into a huge trash can. Suddenly I feel an overwhelming urge for honey-coated popcorn. I console myself when the officer does not mention a fine for my wrongdoing.

We drive circles around town, searching for a place to camp. The exhaustion finally overtakes us all - I stall the Jeep, Warren and Sara have not been talking for hours, and Rob drops the Harley multiple times.

When he drops it right in the middle of town on a paved road, he gives up. Rob makes no attempt to move, and just sits on the ground next to it. He is so completely exhausted he actually asks me to ride the bike, though I'm certain I will fare much worse. Together, the three of us heave it to the shade, where we collapse in silence for ten minutes, trying to right ourselves.

Eventually, we find a satisfactory campground before melting in the shower as the road grime is washed away. The lure of shiny things is too great, so after relaxing all afternoon and drinking huge amounts of water, we wander into town to see what is on offer. At the sight of pizza and beer we get a little carried away, and spend more on our first night in Chile than in three weeks in Bolivia.

After all we have shared, it's hard to believe we part ways in the morning, never to meet again.

Ψ   Ψ   Ψ

Without a doubt this is the kind of adventure I have been searching for during the entire journey, maybe even my entire life.

This has been an expedition.

Bolivia has the most stunning and unique landscapes, unlike anything I have seen on this planet. On the salt flats and further South there was no safety net and absolutely no room for error. We were far off the track, forced to think on our feet, living every minute.

I have never felt more alive.

I'm thoroughly addicted and I want more.

When Things Go Wrong

Alaska and Argentina
2009, 2011

C OMMONLY people plan and prepare for a trip like mine as if it were a space shuttle mission. Tens of thousands of hours and dollars are spent planning for every possible contingency and people bring enough equipment for a large army - including the proverbial kitchen sink. This is a mistake. So much planning removes spontaneity and adventure from the expedition. It also sets up extremely stressful situations when everything does not go according to the million dot-point-plan.

Consider the following times on my expedition when things went 'wrong'. Many people would find these situations unacceptable and stressful. Had I spent more time and money planning, I probably could have avoided both. Personally, I think they're a part of the experience not to be missed.
I will let you decide.

Coolant Drain

The plastic drain plug on the bottom of the radiator has dripped since I flushed it before starting the trip. In Valdez Alaska, I notice more than the usual few drops, so I try to tighten it for the tenth time using my hand. It won't budge, so I get a large wrench and try again. Now with more leverage, I snap off the plastic plug. The slow drip is now gushing, and I scramble to duct tape a rag over it while I improvise a plan.

A local saw my boneheaded move and suggests a garage a couple of miles down the highway. The owner John is a friendly local who should be able to help. Terrified of overheating the engine, I watch the temperature gauge like a hawk. On the drive it never moves from center, making me feel a little better.

I explain my genius move to John, who immediately understands my predicament and wants to help. Unfortunately he is extremely busy and his entire shop is full. It will be a few days until he can look at it, he says.

What he does suggest, however, is that I can work on it myself right there in his gravel parking lot. He is even happy to lend me anything I might need. We talk around it for a while before he convinces me to take out the whole radiator and fish out the broken pieces of plastic plug. While it's only plastic, there is a good chance it will eventually find it's way into the water pump where it might cause real damage. As John rightly points out, it's much better to deal with it now than when it breaks something on the side of the road in Honduras.

I borrow a bucket and drain the entire cooling system before removing the radiator in about forty-five minutes. I take my time so I will remember how it goes back together. I can easily see the plastic pieces sitting neatly in the bottom of the radiator, just as John said they would be. After flushing with water and blowing everything out with John's air hose, I'm satisfied I got all the pieces and there is no chance of damage later.

In need of a replacement plug, John assures me I can hitchhike into town. On the highway the first car stops when I stick out my thumb. Soon I'm chatting madly to Rick, a guy who came to Valdez thirty-five years ago for one summer and never left. He absolutely loves Alaska, and talks a mile a minute on the short ride into town.

I buy a replacement plug at NAPA, and again the first car picks me up, even before I have walked to the highway. Michelle also came here a handful of years ago to look around for the summer, and also has never left. Once again, she raves about how friendly everyone is and how strong the Alaskan community is. She can't imagine ever going back South, it's just too crazy there she says.

Back at John's shop I quickly install the replacement plug, put everything back together and refill the coolant. Standing in front of John's shop, watching the endless Northern sunset creep across the sky we each crack a beer from the case I bought to say thanks. John explains how much he loves the place, and how he also came to Alaska for just one summer many, many years ago. It's so beautiful, and the people so genuine and friendly, he simply never left.
He is now clearly proud to call himself an Alaskan.

It's clear Alaska is remarkable, as are the people who call it home.

Gas Drain

I'm in Southern Argentina, on the world famous Route 40. Distances are huge, so I deliberately fill the tank until I see gas sitting at the cap, full to the last drop. I ask around and I'm assured I will find gas stations on my planned route. With no reason to worry I thoroughly enjoy the gorgeous sunny drive through the massive glacier-capped mountains of Patagonia. After about three hundred miles I pull into the tiny town of *Bajo Caracoles* soon after the gas warning light has flashed on.

Inside the gas station, the owner does not even look at me during the following conversation, which follows a now familiar South American trend:

"Hi, can I buy some gas please?"
"There is none."
"Oh, when will there be more?"
"I don't know."
"When does gas usually come?"
"I don't know."
"What day does it normally come?"
"I don't know."
"Should I wait here until tomorrow?"
"I don't know."
"So, what can I do about getting gas?"
"I don't know."
"Do you think there is gas in the next town?," I ask hopefully.
"Of course there is," he replies condescendingly, as if I asked a stupid question.

As I have found common in South America, this man knows absolutely nothing about his own situation but is an expert on a town sixty miles away.

My choices are clear - I can sit around with my new 'outgoing' friend, waiting for the remote possibility of gas to arrive, or I can hit the road and at least get closer to a town that definitely might have some. The warning light on the Jeep indicates forty miles remaining, though I know it's conservative. I'm confident there is more in the tank than the gauge indicates. Combined with the knowledge there are only twenty-five miles of gravel before a new paved road starts, I think I can pull off fifty-five miles.
Sixty if it's downhill.

I see no point in waiting any longer, so I set off with the near certainty of running out of gas before the next station, eighty miles distant. I feel strange to be driving the Jeep knowing I'm likely to run out of gas. On one hand I'm moving closer to a station that probably has gas, while on the other I'm closer to almost certain failure. I take hypermiling to the next level, coasting with barely my little toe on the pedal. To entertain myself I count down the number of miles remaining out loud. For the first twenty miles the gauge continues to fall, before it hits rock bottom, physically unable to move lower.

I pass the fifty-five mile mark, then sixty in total disbelief. Sixty-five miles rolls by and a tiny speck of hope creeps in. If I can just make seventy-five miles, I'm basically there. I clear my throat to announce only five miles remain, though before I can utter a sound the engine completely dies.
No coughing. No spluttering. Completely dead.
I can only hope it didn't suck up gunk that is surely lurking at the bottom of the tank.

In the now pitch-dark and moonless night I roll into the ditch and setup camp, digging myself in to wait for the new day. I have to smile - in my all adventures and years of driving, this is the first time I have ever run out of gas.
Tomorrow is sure to be interesting.

Ψ   Ψ   Ψ

I eat a quick breakfast at dawn before standing with my thumb out. In less than three minutes the first car of the day - a chatty Frenchman in a rental - stops to pick me up. He loves Patagonia, and has about nine video cameras to record every second of his adventure. His enthusiasm is infectious, and I soon realize he loves this place more than I do. I can't help notice the last three miles into town are all downhill - I really did almost make it.

The station has plenty of gas, and the smiling attendant finds and cleans a one gallon container for me to borrow, no problem at all.

Less than five minutes later I'm walking back on the main road and before I even put up my thumb a car swings around on the edge of town. The locals explain they saw the Jeep in the ditch, so I'm a dead giveaway carrying the gas container. Knowing what it feels like to run out of gas, they wanted to help. Talk about friendly.

When the Jeep fires up without a problem my new friends wave as their old Ford Escort rattles away in a cloud of smoke.

For almost two years I have thought the tank is bigger than the official nineteen gallons, though try as I might at the station, I can't get a drop more than eighteen gallons in.

Ψ   Ψ   Ψ

Looking back, I have to smile at the worry and fear surrounding breaking down or running out of gas. For many Overlanders these events are seen as complete failure and must be avoided at all costs. Many people go to great lengths to carry an enormous quantity of tools, spare parts and gas in at attempt to prevent the 'ordeals' I experienced. Severely overloaded vehicles often have multiple steel jerry cans on the roof. I have never met anyone that actually used them, they just carry them around full all the time. Some people even spend thousands trying to source maps showing every single gas station on their route.

In reality, problems are all about attitude. If you want it to be an ordeal, it will be. On the other hand, if you keep a smile on your face and have patience, they can be no problem at all and provide a great excuse to get out of the vehicle and interact with friendly locals where you otherwise would not have.

Some even say it's not an expedition until things go wrong.

On Debt

S OON after driving into Mexico I started to wonder what was going on. Even on weekdays, thousands of people laze around, apparently enjoying huge amounts of leisure time. They're on the beach playing guitar, cooking, eating, laughing and enjoying time with their families. None appear stressed or worried about the time. Everyone apparently has ample time to stop and chit-chat on the street. Even when I buy things like tacos or gas, the store keepers are in no rush, and would rather chat than take my money.
Work is just not a priority.

All appear fit and able-bodied and as far as I can see, people do this every day. This is in stark contrast to the world I have lived in for my entire life, and the polar-opposite of fast-paced North America I have just left.

Why don't these people have to go to work?

Why are people so relaxed?
How can they have so much leisure time?

I searched for answers to these questions all throughout Latin America. I had no idea why so many people do not *need* to get up every morning and trundle off to work, just as I had done.

It took the entire two years to finally understand what was really going on.

Ψ   Ψ   Ψ

It was actually a Russian I met in Southern Argentina who finally explained it to me. Like a slap in the face, it became crystal clear that Latin America makes perfect sense and it's actually 'our' world that is dysfunctional.

"Everyone has heard the story of the horse pulling the cart with a carrot dangling in front of his nose," Alexsi says.
"The carrot tricks the horse into pulling the cart all day, and the master will eventually give him the carrot when the work is done."
"It's common to think the horse is stupid, because he keeps walking and walking even though he will never reach the carrot."
"Very few people have the faintest clue what that story is about, or the moral lesson we should learn from it."

"In *your* world," he continues, "people can have anything they want, right now. A new big-screen phone, a laptop or even an all-inclusive vacation. There is a store on literally every corner offering a fantastic deal. People walk in, sign some paperwork, and walk out five minutes later with that shiny new product."
"Billions have been spent to make the entire process as quick and easy as possible," he says with a grin.

"The shiny new product could even be a car - the high price makes no difference to the buying experience. A person just has to sign on the dotted line and it's theirs. It really is that easy. Right away they can show off their new purchase to their friends, getting gratification almost instantly. It's now even common to congratulate someone on their purchase, like it's some kind of achievement to sign a piece of paper."

"Sadly, the amount of work they will have to put in for the gratification they are already getting is not at all clear."

"What hardly anyone in your world understands," he goes on, "is the crushing debt and years of payments they will have for the instant gratification. Most people don't even understand they have a loan for their cellphone. They have no idea their 'monthly fee' includes paying off the phone itself. The marketing material says *'Free Phone'* and people simply believe it."

"The phone - and all other credit purchases - would quickly be repossessed if monthly payments stop," he concludes.

"Without fully being aware of it, these people must now work for many hours to pay-off a reward they already have. It's likely they will still be making payments long after it has become obsolete and outdated - or worse, broken or stolen."

"The burden is much bigger when spending larger sums of money on a big screen TV or new car."

"Unlike the hard working horse, the majority of people in your world take the reward before putting in the work."

"Borrowing huge sums of money means the work-reward cycle is backwards."

$$\Psi \quad \Psi \quad \Psi$$

"In *this* world," Alexi gestures around with his hands, "virtually nobody can get a loan. For all intents and purposes, there are no credit cards, there are no payment plans and there are no car loans. The economy is simply not strong and stable enough to allow it. If someone does not have the cash, they can not have the shiny thing they want."

"Like the horse, people here **must** do the work before they can enjoy the reward."

"When a young person *here* wants a new iPhone, she must go to work and save the money. Buying a new iPhone upfront is not cheap, but a new iPhone can make her cool, so she thinks she will save and buy one with cash."
"It takes many hours of work to earn that much money, and it's difficult to put it aside as savings, always waiting to enjoy her hard work. While slaving at work this young lady will see her family and friends enjoying their days - playing guitar, hanging out on the beach and playing with their younger relatives."

"Very quickly, anyone with half a brain will realize a new iPhone is not worth all those hours slaving at work. So they quit their job, and go back to playing guitar and hanging out with family and friends on the beach."

"The simple truth is that once a person has food and shelter - and maybe a little recreation money - they really don't **need** to go to work anymore, so they don't."

"When they must put in the hard work before enjoying the reward, almost everyone quickly sees that pulling the heavy cart for all those hours is really not worth a tiny carrot," Alexi says, now smiling broadly.

"Because everything is in the correct order, people here clearly understand the relationship between the amount of work they must put in, and the reward they will get for it."

$$\Psi \quad \Psi \quad \Psi$$

"People in your world are setting themselves up to be miserable," Alexi continues.
"They pile on debt, while enjoying the rewards instantly. Then they are forced to spend decades slaving at work to pay for it all. Unfortunately, they have literally no choice. Even if a new child comes along, or the person decides they would rather go

back to University or one of a million other life choices, they **must** keeping paying for the stuff they got, even when it's old or broken."

"They have finished eating the carrot a long, long time ago, and yet they must continue to pull the heavy cart - often, with no end in sight."

"Because the reward came before the work, the amount of work required for a given reward is fuzzy and unclear."
"Worse still, they are now locked in."

"If they decide the amount of work required to pay for the reward is too much, they can not change their mind. Because they ate the carrot first, they **must** continue going to work. They are literally trapped."

"To me, that is the definition of unhappiness; pulling a heavy cart with the full understanding there is no reward at the end."

Ψ   Ψ   Ψ

"So you see, the horse is actually clever," Alexi says, grinning again.
"He does the hard work, then enjoys the carrot as reward at the end."
"Any time he decides the carrot is not a big or juicy enough reward for the distance he is pulling the heavy cart, he can simply stop."

"If he ate the carrot before doing the work he would be miserable."

"Be careful about bringing debt into your life Dan," he finishes. "It can quickly trap you in a life with little reward."

"When you are not saddled with debt, you will find you actually don't need to go to work a great deal and you will be free to enjoy life with your friends and family, playing guitar and hanging out on the beach."

The Southern Patagonian Icefield

Mount Fitz Roy Region, Patagonia
March 2011

I spend a couple of sunny days relaxing in *El Calafate*, resupplying and recharging my batteries. The town and surroundings are staggeringly beautiful, causing me to literally stop and stare whenever I turn a corner and am greeted with another jaw-dropping view.

Randomly, I cross paths with Sonny, a backpacker from Lithuania who is traveling Patagonia as part of a photography contest he won. It's not every day I meet someone from Lithuania - actually Sonny is the first - and I thoroughly enjoy hearing his world perspective. Photography is also quickly becoming one of my biggest passions so it's fantastic to learn from someone who is obviously so accomplished.

Sonny is a serious high-altitude mountaineer, and we talk for hours about some of his bigger summits. On one climb,

Sonny had a fall and slid many hundreds of yards on the steep and snowy slope completely out of control. Not roped to his climbing companions, they could only watch in horror. By some miracle, he was able to stop his slide with his ice axe, less than a hundred yards from a cliff that would have been certain death.

On another climb in remote Central Asia, Sonny woke in the tent to discover one of his climbing partners had died overnight. The extremely high elevation and lack of oxygen had slowly and silently suffocated his friend. With nothing to be done, he and the third climber continued to the summit, a massive 24,750 ft.
With Sonny's guidance, the authorities later retrieved the body with a helicopter.

Sonny's stories blow my mind. Being so close to death is extremely confronting and feels way outside my comfort zone. I'm convinced I could never attempt such a feat and I'm certain high altitude mountaineering is not for me. Sonny just shrugs and says death is part of it. You either learn to accept it, or you quit the sport. He then proudly shows off his badly disfigured toes - victims of severe frostbite on yet another climb.

$$\Psi \quad \Psi \quad \Psi$$

We're both excited to see the enormous *Perito Moreno* glacier, though neither of us is excited about the $50 USD per person entry fee. Always the cheapskates, we decide Sonny should hide in the rear storage box of the Jeep while I drive in. The box is tiny and I feel terrible closing the rear tailgate on Sonny, though he insists he is fine.

The guy selling tickets at the gate wants to chat, and it's more than fifteen minutes before I can pull over to let Sonny out. I have been calling out to him for the last five minutes with no reply, and I'm genuinely concerned he has suffocated. When I finally open the rear hatch, Sonny smiles out at me. As I help him climb out, he insists he is fine and simply could not hear me.

The glacier is everything we hoped for and we spend most of the day relaxing in the warm sunshine, chatting back and forth. Every few minutes enormous chunks of ice calve off a hundred yards in front of us, which is extremely loud and impressive. After waiting many hours we finally tear ourselves away and are less than fifty yards into the trees when we hear the crowd erupt with cheers for a massive calving event.
You can't win them all.

In the afternoon we race to the summit of the nearby *Cerro Crystal*, with Sonny's superior fitness quickly shining through. He strides confidently to the top without even breathing hard, while I puff and pant my way slowly behind.
At the top we make a deal - this will not be the last mountain we summit together.

Ψ   Ψ   Ψ

The following day we set out with loaded hiking packs to explore the area around mighty *Mt. Fitz Roy*, 11,235ft. and equally impressive *Cerro Torre*, 10,262ft. - notoriously difficult to summit even in the best of weather. We don't have a specific destination in mind, but we're certain we will find adventure and spectacular views.

Over a few days we hike from *Laguna Torre* all the way to *Laguna De Los Tres* at the extreme Northern limit of the park. Eventually we double-back on ourselves, hiking most trails in the area more than once. We're up every morning before sunrise with our cameras and fall into our tents late at night after star photos. With apparently limitless patience, Sonny is happy to answer all my photography questions and teaches me a lot in a short time.

Mt. Fitz Roy is famous for it's 'Red Flash' sunrise, an ideal photography opportunity. When my alarm sounds at 4.30am, I simply can't summon the courage to leave my warm sleeping bag, so I roll over and go right back to sleep. Sonny hikes the hour and a half to the viewing area and enjoys the famous sunrise in solitude, before we hike over fifteen hours with full packs for the day.

Wow, this guy is dedicated.

At *Laguna Hija* we take a refreshing swim before sunning ourselves on the pebble beach. At glacier *Piedras Blancas* (white rocks) we eat chunks of recently calved million-year-old ice. Although we hear the glacier cracking and moving, we don't see any major action from our distant vantage point.

We thoroughly enjoy the three day hiking circuit, and neither of us wants it to end.

Ψ   Ψ   Ψ

Back at the Ranger station we sign in before cooking lunch and resupplying our packs with food from the Jeep. We register again at the Ranger station and hit the trail to *Laguna Toro*. The trail is marked variously as taking between six and seven hours, though both Sonny and I fancy ourselves as faster than average. The hike winds through breathtaking forests, across lush farmland and finishes with a long, long descent to the valley bottom.

Arriving in camp foot-sore and tired after four and a half hours, we feel like winners.

To my surprise, Sonny has carried a bottle of red wine in a coke bottle. It only makes sense to lighten his load, so we down the lot before crawling into our respective tents soon after dark. I'm utterly exhausted, and sleep like a rock.

Still rubbing sleep from our eyes at seven the next morning, we find ourselves staring at a lively glacier-melt river. After scouting up and downstream trying to waste time, we both give in to the inevitable. We string our boots over our shoulders and plunge into the freezing whitewater. We cross multiple braided streams, the first couple of which are small and only ankle deep. These do not sting too much. Slowly but surely, the cumulative effect kicks in - the more time we spend in the icy water, the worse our feet get. Walking with numb feet is not actually the problem, it's the searing pain that comes immediately after as the blood rushes back into my feet. Walking on the sharp rocks and pebbles in this state is not enjoyable, though I can't help but laugh at our comical hobbling - a cross between old men walking gingerly and youngsters hopping about.

About halfway into a knee deep crossing I see large chunks of glacier ice float past on their way downstream.
I knew the water was seriously cold, but this is crazy!

Sitting on the rocky shore I rub my feet vigorously to encourage blood flow and work away the painful tingling. I'm happy to put on dry socks before I move quickly to warm up my core.

We make great time, though in our haste we lose the faint trail. We're forced to find our own way down at the region where glacier turns to lake. I'm in awe as we walk next to and even under the enormous towering glaciers. Eventually, fed up with the slow going, Sonny leads us up onto the flat surface of *Tunel Glacier*. With Sonny's experience I feel confident striding quickly along and am fascinated to have a good look down into the crevasses he points out as we go.
I can not see the bottom of most.

I'm completely awe-struck by the expanse of ice stretching endlessly when we arrive at the high point of the ominously named *Paso Del Viento* (Pass of the wind). The view in every direction is of pure ice, with beautiful swirls and patterns caused by millions of years of slowly marching forward. Second in the world only to Southeastern Alaska's St. Elias Chugach Icefield, The Southern Patagonian Icefield is 6,500 square miles of pure ice. The Ranger station had a 3D model of the entire icefield, showing what looked like an arm with many fingers. I'm staggered to realize what I can see now is only one of the many 'fingers'. Although I can see nothing but ice stretching to the horizon, it's only a tiny fraction of the whole. The ice in front of me which takes up my entire field of vision is insignificant in comparison to the main bulk, many miles distant and out of sight.

The wind whipping off the ice is bitingly cold, though thankfully not too strong. We stay as long as we can bear it, trying to soak in the enormity of the view. Clouds have been rolling in all morning, though they do nothing to diminish the spectacle laid out in front of us. I'm so determined to stay as long as possible I run on the spot to stay warm.

Finally we tear ourselves away and begin the long trek down to our waiting tents. During the hike I formulate a master plan to cross the glacier-melt river and become fixated on avoiding the unpleasantries of the morning. I will admit simply taking off my socks and plunging in with my boots on is not much of a plan. Not surprisingly, it doesn't help much.

After a nine hour hike most people choose to stay the night in camp. Always looking to push, Sonny and I are in the mood for more. After feasting on the remainder of our food, we hoof it all the way back to *El Chaltén* and the waiting Jeep. Extremely foot-sore and a little cold we arrive just after dark. The fours hours of mostly uphill slogging was exhausting, but we love beating our own time.

Ψ   Ψ   Ψ

I feel lucky to have bumped into Sonny and spent time at the immense Southern Patagonian Icefield. The hike in was difficult and I was often cold, though the reward was again well worth the effort.

I can't help but wonder how many years the icefield will last. To this day it remains one of the most unique natural wonders I have ever seen.

The Jeep

A s a teenager I daydreamed about driving a Jeep with no roof and no doors to exotic locations - who didn't! Living next to the mighty Canadian Rockies in Calgary was the perfect time to get one and I folded the roof down for my first test drive. Just eight years old, completely stock, and with no optional features, the little four-cylinder Jeep Wrangler was everything I dreamed of.

I repeatedly drove into the Rockies on camping trips, leaving the roof and doors at home. From sun and wind burn to freezing cold rain, I was living the Jeep dream.
I loved every second.

As the idea for the trip formed in my mind, I felt increasingly certain it was the perfect vehicle for the job. Because it is so small the Jeep is extremely capable off-road and it's not too bad on gas consumption, being a four-cylinder. Weekend camping trips on remote logging roads provide perfect practice to build confidence in the Jeep, my camping setup and my self-reliance.

I loved the soft-top, and wanted to complete the journey with it. My dream included driving to beaches in Costa Rica and over mountain passes in the Andes with no roof or doors. I knew that if someone really wanted to get inside, they could simply cut the canvas with a knife. Replacing or repairing the canvas would likely be problematic, and so to counter this, I simply never locked the doors.

That's right - for the entire journey, the front doors of the Jeep were never locked.

I needed a way to keep things like my passport, credit cards, camera and laptop safe, so my brother and I spent a weekend building a locking storage box. It's a simple plywood shelf that makes a large secure box when the rear tailgate is locked with the key. This $60 USD box is the only modification I make to my Jeep to prepare it for the trip.

Early on - through Alaska and North America - the Jeep was just a tool. I used it to get where I wanted, then I got out and did some activity like hiking. It was fantastic, though it was just a vehicle. Somewhere in Central America my feelings towards the Jeep began to change. Driving in foreign countries, far outside my comfort zone, I started to feel like the Jeep was my home and sanctuary. Although I always drive with the windows down and only a canvas roof, I felt safe inside the Jeep, regardless of the chaos outside.

Everything I need when camping is accessed via the rear tailgate, so I develop a habit of pitching my tent directly behind the Jeep. Often I sit to cook meals in my chair between it and my tent, and often I thought of this space as my living room. Despite the constantly changing world around me, I had a stable living space. I felt a sense of relief each morning when the Jeep was the first thing I saw after unzipping my tent.

Somewhere along the way, I begin to talk out loud to the Jeep. When uncertain of a turn, or trying to decide between a side road or the direct route, I often consult my trustworthy companion. With no GPS or electronic navigation of any kind, getting lost becomes a way of life in the monster South American cities. As one example I spent more than three hours trying to *leave* Quito in Ecuador. Completing a trip like this with nothing more than paper maps sounds romantic, though it can also be burdensome. In fact, navigating eventually became the most stressful part of my daily life.

When really struggling, having a reliable companion to consult is always helpful, and with the help of the Jeep we always got through. I would list the options out loud, and gently tap the dash board, asking for input. In the cities we would fumble our way more-or-less South, while out in the countryside the Jeep would always choose the tiniest roads possible. With that as our navigation strategy we would set off together in complete agreement.

Ψ   Ψ   Ψ

The Jeep also happens to be the perfect conversation starter. Police and Military roadblocks are never boring, and the Jeep often attracts more attention than me. Seeing a strong 4x4 in a small package, locals are drawn to it. They immediately ask if it's for sale or if I will give it away. I explain the engine size, four wheel drive and excellent reliability. The map of the Americas on the hood helps immensely to explain where I'm coming from and where I'm going.

Talking about the Jeep to locals on the roadside also improves my Spanish leaps and bounds. Early on my vocabulary was dominated by words related to the Jeep, and my journey. To this day when I dream in Spanish, I'm often talking about my little Jeep.

Family is a huge part of life in Latin America, and so inevitably

Police and Military ask where my wife and kids are. Without fail they are shocked to learn I don't have either. It's clearly difficult for them to understand why a man my age would not have a family. At first jokingly, and then more and more seriously, I point to the Jeep and say:
"She is my girlfriend," which is always met with genuine laughter.

Without knowing it I had stumbled on a fantastic way to break the ice and ease any thoughts of bribery or hassle. In fact, I'm certain that more than once I saw a little envy in their eyes - I only have a Jeep in my life, rather than a wife and all that might entail. I think more than a few guys would have gladly swapped places.

On one memorable occasion, this joking approach went wrong in the most hilarious way. Always open to the idea of passengers, I pick up a Swedish backpacker in Colombia. The backpacker has the stereotypical blue eyes and long blond hair you might guess. Military roadblocks in Colombia can sometimes be serious, and together we stop at one manned by well-armed men dressed head-to-toe in full combat fatigues. While getting my papers, I point to the Jeep and deliver my standard line, "She is my girlfriend."

The heavily-armed officer gives me a peculiar look before quickly waving me away, clearly wanting nothing more to do with me.

Only later do I realize he thought I was talking about the large bearded man in the passenger seat.

$$\Psi \quad \Psi \quad \Psi$$

Over the course of 40,000 miles, the Jeep never broke down once. In my eyes this makes it the perfect vehicle. After all, reliability is more important than anything else when in remote lands far from home. I thoroughly enjoy working on it and I perform all the tire rotations and oil changes myself at the required intervals. I feel a sense of satisfaction after having a good look around at the suspension and drive-line while underneath. The Jeep was designed and built to eat up tens of thousands of miles on rough roads, and it does exactly that.

I'm convinced the perfect reliability record is due in part to having such light gear. Because it's so light the Jeep easily skims over nasty roads without breaking a sweat. This means much less wear and tear on everything from the tires and suspension to the engine and gearbox.

Before setting out, I had no idea how much of a trusty companion my little Jeep would turn out to be. Over time the Jeep took on it's own personality, and became a unique character on the journey. Not only the most important piece of gear I had, it also became my reliable friend and adventure buddy.

While there was often nobody else in the Jeep with me, I never really felt alone.

As for a name - I didn't find one that stuck.
Just 'Jeep'.

.

End Of The Road

Ushuaia, Tierra Del Fuego, Argentina
March 2011

F ROM the day I turned South at the Arctic Ocean in Alaska, I've been watching the growing yellow line on the hood representing my progress through the Americas. It's a great overview of where I have come from, where I am now, and what is immediately in front of me. For the last few months I have been acutely aware I'm running out of map.
There will soon be nowhere left to drive.

Ψ   Ψ   Ψ

Almost two years ago in *Baja California*, Duke and I randomly met Seth and Parker, two brothers riding bicycles on a similar journey from North to South. While camping together in the desert we realized we left Prudhoe Bay within a day of each other, and we have been extremely close ever since. There is a very good chance I passed them on the Alaska Highway, and they leapfrogged me while I was exploring the lower 48 of the USA.

Long after Mexico, I grinned from ear to ear watching them ride into The Secret Garden Cotopaxi, the hostel I managed in Ecuador. There were so many stories of adventure to catch up on, and so much to look forward to. We have kept in touch ever since, with the brothers always about a month in the lead.

To say they inspire me is a huge understatement. Whenever the going is tough, or I'm a little uncertain of the vast unknown ahead, it's reassuring to know they blazed the path.
If they can do it on bikes, surely I can do it.

Now, just before the end of the road in Argentina, we organize to finish our journeys together. This will be our final night camping in the wild, something I'm struggling to comprehend.

Ψ   Ψ   Ψ

I venture off the highway onto gravel, and find the beautiful *Lac Bombilla* nestled in an immense forest of towering pine. Seth and Parker are both fly fishing, and I'm immediately on a high when I spot them on shore. Soon we're laughing, reminiscing and telling crazy stories about our respective adventures over the past two years.

We visited many of the same places, though of course we had vastly different experiences. I'm shocked to hear one mountain pass in Southern Ecuador took them three days of hard riding to climb, and remains in their memories as some of the hardest days on the road. After I finally clarify exactly where they are talking about, I remember the Jeep powered uphill in a couple of hours. Because it was so easy in my Jeep, this mountain pass is unremarkable in my memory.

On the other hand the brothers are excited to hear of all my hiking adventures, the complete opposite of their trip.

Whenever off the bikes they would immediately crash and do as little as possible. Hearing about my hiking in Peru has them wishing they could carry hiking packs.

Cold drizzle begins to fall, and although it does not dampen our spirits, our campfire skills are pushed to the limit. After chatting long into the night we succumb to the cold and finally crawl into our tents in the wee hours of the morning. I sense none of us wanted this day to end - we're feeling uncertain about what tomorrow actually means.

Greeted by a warm and sunny day we're immediately in high spirits and excited to hit the road for the final day. After breaking camp I quickly pull away and am once again alone with my thoughts as I climb up and over the final mountain pass. The sunshine entices me to repeatedly stop and pose for photos with the Jeep, which feels like the right thing to do.

I roll into *Ushuaia*, the most Southerly city in the world and the end of the road. On the edge of town I pose for photos in front of the 'Welcome' sign, feeling proud and a little conspicuous. I feel good, but the milestone does not bring forth the emotions I have been expecting. I have just completed the biggest achievement of my life, though I can not bring myself to understand it.

I sit and think for a few minutes before realizing I feel like I'm in any other town along the way. I feel as though I'm just visiting for a few days, and then I will continue, as I have done for almost two years. The constant movement has become so ingrained I realize it will be difficult to convince myself I have finished.
I also have absolutely no idea how I will resume any kind of 'normal' life, whatever that means.

Ushuaia itself is stunningly beautiful. Surrounded on three sides by snow-capped mountains, the picture-perfect view is completed by the stunning ocean dominating the Southern view, dotted with numerous small islands.

I find the only campground in town - *La Pista Del Andio* - a famous haunt in Overlanding circles. Set on a beautiful grassy hill above town, and with many colorful flowers in full bloom it completes the postcard feeling. In the early afternoon sun I wait impatiently for the arrival of the brothers.

For the entire journey I have painted a yellow line on the map on the hood tracking my progress. Tt feels significant to finally finish the line from one extreme end of The Americas to the other. It's now impossible to make the line any longer. My face stretches into a huge grin that will not go away.

When Seth and Parker ride in we kick off a party of immense proportions. After multiple celebration beers and shouts of 'cheers', we move into town to one of the famous all-you-can-eat *Asada* restaurants. Argentinians are famous for their barbecue meat for two reasons - because they love it so much and because it's so good. All manner of delicious meats and organs are slow-cooked to perfection over coals, often taking many hours. Thankfully the all-you-can-eat restaurant is more than happy to fill our plates to the brim many times over. This turns into a friendly competition, and between us we consume a truly staggering amount of meat.

At six foot four, Parker is a big guy, and has been burning over five thousand calories per day for the last eighteen months. He easily takes the crown, and goes back for yet another heaping plate long after Seth and I have tapped out.

Without a moments rest the bar-hopping begins in earnest. We're again bursting with laughter and disbelief as we each recount some of the more outrageous encounters and characters from the road. Many times during the night we say "This is biggest achievement of my life," causing us to stop and ponder what it all means. The topic of effort versus reward continually surfaces, and we all agree the most challenging experiences were also the most rewarding. Beer after beer we continue at a frantic pace, apparently making friends and having a great time.

Ψ   Ψ   Ψ

In the morning there are a lot of sore and confused heads, causing us to tread gingerly. In the early afternoon we return to one bar, hoping to collect a forgotten jacket. The staff roar with laughter at the sight of us and insist we come inside. Although none of us remembers the details, they assure us we were great fun last night, and want to start the party again right now. None of us has the stomach for it, so we gingerly tiptoe away with a promise to return another night.

For the rest of the week we're surprised when people in town recognise us, and even know our names and stories. Apparently we made a lot of friends that night.

Ψ   Ψ   Ψ

Having arrived in *Ushuaia* and held our 'end of the road' party, we start to feel a bit lost. The wilderness surrounding town is supremely beautiful, so we soon come up with a plan.

At the supermarket we load the Jeep with all the camping gear, food and drinks it can carry. Seth and Parker are ecstatic to have me carry luxury items for them like steak and beer - things they have gone without for almost two years. We make our way South to *Tierra Del Feugo National Park*, literally at the end of the road. Seth and Parker insist they must ride their bikes to complete the journey, so I have fun leapfrogging them to take photos.

After finding a beautiful clearing surrounded by small lakes and green grass, we declare camp for a few nights. The next day we celebrate my Birthday by throwing Disc Golf on an improvised course in and around the trees and rocks on the grass. Again we linger, not wanting to actually end what has been the biggest achievement of our lives.

One morning we agree the time has come, and we separately travel the final three miles on the gravel road to the physical end of the road. There are many handshakes, smiles and photos taken in front of the sign that marks the end. Bringing the whole expedition full-circle, I walk into the Southern Ocean, just as I did in the Arctic Ocean.

Something clicks in my mind.
Now I am done.

Hilariously, Parker has me tow him back to camp with a rope behind the Jeep.
"I rode every mile South from Alaska to Argentina," he says with a huge grin.
"I don't need to ride back North!"

Together we have a fantastic few days around the area. I'm extremely happy and thankful to share the end-of-the-road experience with these friends. We're in a unique position to understand each other - and what we have achieved - better than anyone else can.

Ψ   Ψ   Ψ

I feel elated to have achieved my goal, though I also feel conflicted about the unknown that now lies in front of me. For the last two years I have had a clear purpose. Aiming for *Ushuaia* has kept me engaged, focused and busy, all things I need in my life.

Without a clear purpose, I know a feeling of listlessness will soon creep in. Added to that, I own nothing outside the Jeep, and I have no house to 'go back' to.

In fact, I even feel unsure about what country I should live in, let alone what city.

An Adventure Ends

Argentina
April 2011

I RONICALLY, the most difficult part of driving from the top of Alaska to the bottom of South America might actually be selling the Jeep. Selling a foreign-plated vehicle in Argentina turns out to be a lot more difficult that I first thought.

Argentina and Chile both have extremely strict importation laws to protect local producers, making a legal sale virtually impossible. High import taxes in Argentina mean the Jeep is worth many times what I paid for it back in Canada. Because of this, Argentines are feverish to buy it for what seems like a bargain price to them.

I put a 'For Sale' sign in the window, and soon every second local asks about buying it. I have to politely explain that only foreigners can buy it due to the problem of importation laws. Quickly, the locals think up all kinds of crazy - and mostly illegal - ways we can make the sale work.

Most ideas revolve around reporting it stolen, some involve stripping it for parts and even crazier ideas involve various takes on insurance fraud. I'm ready to sell and move onto new things in my life, though I'm not sure I want to risk trouble with the authorities. I would rather do this legally, if at all possible.

After a lot of back-and-forward and planning a strategy, I sign a 'Power of Attorney' for a friendly Argentine. This legal document authorizes him to drive my Jeep in Argentina without me. The story we concoct is that he will drive it for 'a little while', until I 'come back' in a year or so. (cough, cough).

With that document we drive together to the nearby border with Chile. By leaving the country the import papers in my name are cancelled, which is one hurdle down. After lunch in the small town on the other side, we return to Argentina, crossing our fingers. The Argentina Customs officer is clearly not asleep at his post, and he catches onto to our genius plan immediately. He is having none of it, and quickly puts a stop to it.

He becomes irate and is soon talking about arresting the buyer just for driving the foreign-plated Jeep. Sensing failure, I step forward and announce I'm the legal owner and it's not stolen. The Customs officer is now certain of our plan, and explains time and time again the Jeep and I are literally inseparable in Argentina. There is no world where an Argentinian can legally drive it.

Because it has foreign plates, any local caught driving it will go directly to jail. This is not good news.

With no choice I enter Argentina with new paperwork for the Jeep in my name. During this process the Customs officer is rigorous and strictly checks all my papers twice. He makes a public show of looking for some kind of mistake or something to trip me up.

Very quietly and off to the side, he mentions that in two weeks he will be at a near-by remote border station, alone. He suggests it would be an excellent place for us to further discuss the matter of my Jeep, and it's future owner. He assures me we can find a way to make it all 'work out'.

I have come to love the Spanish word *Corrupción*.

Clearly defeated, the supposed buyer and I drive back into Argentina, feeling sorry for ourselves. An hour from the border we are stopped at a routine Police roadblock where my papers are thoroughly scrutinized. Soon multiple officers are searching the Jeep for drugs and anything else they don't like the look of. When the search turns up nothing, they again go back to inspecting my papers. During my many months in Argentina I have never encountered a roadblock like this and I begin to sense something is off.

Eventually the senior officer invites us inside where he directly asks about our intention to import the Jeep into Argentina. It seems our friend back at Customs has called ahead and ordered a good old fashioned shake-down.

This is all a bit funny to us, because we know we have done nothing wrong. After another hour of wasting our time they have no choice and the Police eventually let us proceed.

Ψ   Ψ   Ψ

I give up trying to find creative ways to sell the Jeep to a local, and eventually a solid buyer in *Buenos Aires* surfaces. I consider my options and realize this is my best bet. I hit the road, putting down just over five hundred miles three days in a row, which is way too much.

This prospective buyer is a hilarious Frenchman who has lived in BA for many years. He makes his living online, and because

he earns foreign currency, lives a great life without having to work much at all. Because he is a foreigner, the sale of the Jeep *should* be possible.
Hopefully.

Unfortunately, his Immigration status in Argentina is not exactly 'legal' - he has been here for many years and his three month tourist visa expired long ago. In theory, leaving the country and re-entering should fix the problem - so long as the border officers don't notice the date stamped in his passport when we leave.

We make a plan to take a day cruise to Uruguay, which should be good fun while also solving the Immigration problem. From the little I see of the country, it feels like a laid-back and friendly place, and I wish I could stay longer. This is country number seventeen on the journey, though without the Jeep I'm not sure it counts. Upon re-entry the Frenchman is given a new stamp without hassle. Now there should be nothing stopping him from buying the Jeep.

After talking to Customs and lawyers over and over, we have another 'Power of Attorney' written up. Again our story is that I will just be leaving the country for 'a little while' and my friend will drive it 'until I get back'.
We are both extremely careful never to use the word 'sell' and it seems everyone either believes our story or they just don't care.

We drive to the head Customs office in downtown *Buenos Aires* to finalize the paperwork. It's a surreal moment when all the papers are signed, and the Jeep is legally transferred out of my name. The Argentina Temporary Import is cancelled, and I'm now free to legally leave the country.

Less than fifteen minutes later I book plane tickets, leaving just over twenty-four hours remaining in Latin America. Not for the first time in my life I give away stuff and condense my worldly possessions until they fit in my faithful old backpack.

Ψ   Ψ   Ψ

I jump in the driver's seat for the final time aiming for the airport. I consciously soak in every last minute with my much-loved Jeep, listening to every noise and enjoying every quirk. It has always run perfectly, never once giving a single mechanical issue.

Good Jeep.

For a year and a half I have been saying *"Ella està mi novia"* (She is my girlfriend), and we all know how difficult breakups can be. The Jeep has been the perfect companion on this expedition - and my life - though I feel sure I am doing the right thing. I'm ready for a new life, and I hope my Jeep will have new adventures too.

Just before midnight on April Twelve, 2011, the wheels come to a stop for the final time. I have driven 40,325 miles since leaving Calgary.

The expedition has run a total of six hundred and sixty-seven days. That is one year, nine months and twenty-eight days - twice as long as I originally estimated.

I snap one last photo in front of the Jeep before I wave goodbye and set off to begin a new life.

Ψ   Ψ   Ψ

For the next twenty-nine hours I wait, read, write, think and sleep while moving through different airports, never feeling present anywhere. I transit through Mexico, where Immigration are more than a little suspicious. With dreadlocks and a big beard, I do look slightly homeless.

When I speak passable Spanish, they become genuinely curious. I explain what I have just done, and after a quick bag search they are shaking my hand and congratulation me on visiting so much of Latin America. I can clearly see they are proud I have enjoyed it so thoroughly.

Soon I'm greeted by my always-grinning brother and his girl-friend, holding a huge 'Welcome Home' banner they made. It even has a hand-drawn Jeep and the expedition route drawn on a map. Together, we cross the final border of the expedition. When I left, I honestly thought I was never coming back.

The familiar words uttered by the friendly Immigration officer make me realize how much I have missed this place.
I think I'll stay for a while.

"Welcome to Canada."

Thanks

A N expedition like mine is not a solo operation. Behind the scenes many friends and family were helping with planning, logistics and support. They sent odds and ends through the mail and helped research when I had little or no Internet access.

Most importantly, they were always there to offer support and encouragement when I needed it most.

It's not an exaggeration to say I could not have done it without their help.

The following people were crucial to the success of my expedition, and I owe them huge thanks for helping me live my dream.

– Melissa & Reg for giving me a home before I even began.

– Cal & the whole crew at Northern Reforestation.

– Thomas & Roland - *"What you can dream, you can achieve."*

- Brett & Eva in Whitehorse. A huge thank you.
- Bill, Hans and the whole Whitehorse crew.
- My brother Mike for helping shape my dreams.
- David & Barbara for all their support and encouragement.
- Judy & Kirby for their WCT stories and support.
- Shane & Amy for making me think. Really think.
- Jeff & Andy and the whole Portland crew - awesome time.
- Jen, Greg & Christopher for teaching me about family life.
- My second family in CA for a home away from home.
- Mum & Dad for encouraging me every step of the way.
- Bari for putting up with me.
- Duke for being the perfect partner in crime.
- Kyle in *La Manzanilla* for everything.
- Victor in *Tehuantepec* for a 'family' Christmas.
- Caroline in *Puerto Escondido*. Dreams can be lived!
- Kate for trusting me enough to jump aboard.
- Mike, the hitch-hiking backpacker.
- Vince & Marie for their help, support and inspiration.
- Tarquin, Katherine & the whole Secret Garden crew.
- Seth & Parker for continually inspiring me.
- My sister Liz, my biggest supporter, full of encouragement.
- Mark in NZ - helping from the other side of the world.
- Brendan in Canada for all the support.

This book would not exist without my friend Pete, who inspired and continually encouraged me to write it. It would not be what it is without the tireless editing of my family, especially my Mum.

To research and plan your own global Overland Expedition, checkout *http://wikiOverland.org*[9] which contains everything from routes and budgets to paperwork and gas and diesel prices for every country in the world.

---

[9] *WikiOverland - The Community Encyclopedia of Overland Travel*

Afterword

Returning to The Developed World after two years is not an easy transition. I almost fall over when I walk into Walmart, so staggered am I with the sheer number of items available. I realize that in five minutes here I can buy what took days to find in Argentina - when I was lucky. I see an iPad for the first time in my life and genuinely think I'm in the future.

I'm stunned by the sheer amount of *stuff* people have in this world. From new cars and huge houses to snowboards, quad bikes, kayaks, trailers, RVs, laptops, big TVs, phones...the list goes on.
The idea that people have so much stuff they pay to store it is obscene, and I simply can not understand it.

I also notice how busy everyone is. They have so little time for each other. Virtually nobody stops on the street to chat, and everyone walks at break-neck pace. Work is clearly more important than life.

I struggle to understand this "Land Of Plenty" as I have come to call it.

Ψ   Ψ   Ψ

I sign-up for a desk job, and have the shock of my life realizing this is what I used to do. For eight hours a day I can only look out the window at the beautiful sunshine and mountains. I must sit inside killing time in endless meetings or shuffling emails - toeing the Corporate line.

Everyone around me thinks this life is perfectly normal, and I think it's completely insane.

I drive a $450 car, ride a $30 bike to work and use an old 'dumb' phone a friend gives me.
I open a savings account.

I distract myself after work and on weekends. In the summer I hike and mountain bike, in the winter I snowboard my heart out. I cram in adventures all over Alaska and Yukon, ranging into the Arctic Circle repeatedly. My love of the outdoors grows stronger each day, and I have the time of my life.

Ψ   Ψ   Ψ

Within six months, the whole expedition feels like a dream. Nobody around me can relate to the adventure, so I stop talking and thinking about it.

After a year, I know I have been assimilated into work life when it feels more normal than expedition life.

Often I wake in my apartment disoriented and mumbling in Spanish, trying to remember where I have set up my tent.

I have to look at my own photos and read my own website to convince myself the expedition was real.

While I struggle, I live vicariously through my friends Vince and Marie, who I shared a container with from Panama to Colombia. They conclude their round-the-world expedition by shipping their Land Rover to a new continent and driving home to France.

Vince writes their blog in French, so I follow along using Google Translate. The poorly translated English only adds to how profoundly his writing impacts me.

I will never forget one particular update from Vince:

> *There is something about the earth here.*
> *I can feel it in my bones.*
> *This is where I come from.*
> *Africa is where I come from.*

Ψ   Ψ   Ψ

Time flies.

One year turns into two. Then three. Then four.

I feel recharged, and my dreams take shape, bigger than ever.

I'm ready for another expedition.

Printed in Great Britain
by Amazon